Water Ways

Christine Richardson

Brayford Pool, Lincoln

Water Ways

A Day Drive Guide to
Twenty-Two Rivers and Canals
in South and West Yorkshire,
the North Midlands
and Lincolnshire

CHRISTINE RICHARDSON

The **Hallamshire** Press
1995

1995 © Christine Richardson

Published by The Hallamshire Press
The Hallamshire Press is an imprint of
Interleaf Productions Limited
Exchange Works
Sidney Street
Sheffield S1 3QF
England

Typeset by Interleaf Productions Limited
Printed in Great Britain by
The Cromwell Press, Wiltshire

British Library Cataloguing in Publication Data

Richardson, Christine
 Water Ways:Day Drive Guide to Twenty-two
 Rivers and Canals in South and West
 Yorkshire, the North Midlands and
 Lincolnshire
 I. Title
 386.09428

 ISBN 1-874718-08-3

Contents

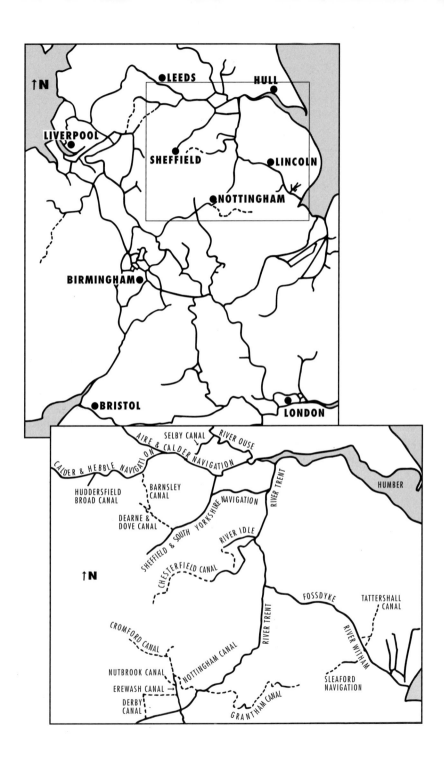

Introduction

THIS book is a day-drive guide to twenty-two waterways in the south of Yorkshire, the North Midlands and Lincolnshire: where to find them, and what can be seen. It is an introduction to a world often by-passed, but nevertheless fascinating and restful. Some waterways are busy with boats, others are quiet, a heartening number are being restored.

There are many sights to see. All sorts of vessels—sea-going ships, canal narrowboats, cruisers, cargo-carrying barges, and yachts. On land there are busy locks, lift-bridges, wharves, quiet towpaths and villages. The wildlife includes kingfishers, herons, cormorants and grebes. Signs of the past are everywhere—bridges with rope-marks on them, old warehouses and stables, rope-rollers and mills.

In Britain we have 2,000 miles of quiet canals and river navigations, linked together to form an intricate system that reaches most parts of our island. Some waterways are well known, at least by name. Others receive little publicity, and reserve their inconspicuous treasures for those who take the time to find them, and many do—walkers, boaters, anglers, artists, photographers, bird-watchers, local historians, and those who enjoy the national pastime of looking at boats.

Waterways can be many things: quiet, reclusive remnants of another age; restful leisure facilities of today; liquid highways carrying heavy cargoes. The waterways are well worth a visit.

The old South Basin, Horncastle

General Description

They were once the trading arteries of the nation, but now the waterways are valued for their leisure potential. Car parks and picnic sites are being created, information panels installed, leaflets issued, and walking routes organised. Pubs and restaurants are realising the importance of waterside sites. Boats are being hired and purchased.

The accompanying towpaths provide a flat route through countryside and city, the varied environment is home to many types of birds, animals and plants. On the navigable waterways boats are another source of interest, the passage of a lock always a highlight.

In hilly Derbyshire the towpaths give easy access to scenery that could otherwise be viewed only after a strenuous walk. Even though road and rail often share the same strategic valleys, it is surprising how quiet waterways such as the **Cromford Canal** remain, hidden from the modern world, their existence is known only to those who have discovered them. In flat Lincolnshire, canals such as the **Grantham** are more remote, the land not dictating the course of surrounding transport systems. Here the waterways have a timeless air about them; very different from the **Trent**, the spine of the local waterway system, which is often lined by flood-meadows. Roads, trains and houses keep a strategic distance from a river that sometimes needs extra room when winter rains and high tides coincide, but when the Trent is behaving itself, the towpath lines the bankside meadows.

Because of their very nature, waterways are dependent on the seasons and the weather. After the series of dry years at the end of the 1980s, the rivers and canals looked a sorry sight, only the minimum of water lining the channels. Normally, however, after a wet winter the feeder streams and reservoirs are full and the waterways look their best in the following spring. April, May and June are good months to see the waterbirds: nests, ducklings, and adults in fine plumage. Boat activity is more evident during the summer, especially in the school holidays, giving extra colour to places such as Torksey at the end of the **Fossdyke** where all sorts of craft may be seen on the visitor moorings. Winter is in some ways the best time to explore the unnavigable canals, such as the **Derby**; foliage that may otherwise obliterate the towpath dies down, and hidden features such as tunnel entrances and old wharves and locks can be seen more clearly.

The Waterways System

In this area the central link in the network is the River Trent, flowing east and north, meeting the Ouse to form the Humber estuary. Throughout history the **Trent** has been a major water highway—playing its part in invasions, the Roman road network, and the Civil War. As a transport system, the river gave coastal shipping access to inland areas, and it carried river barges to various trading towns. Today the Trent still carries cargoes and also has a vital role in draining vast tracts of the North Midlands.

From the Trent the river's tributaries reach out to a wider area and form the oldest arms of the system—in the past creating inland ports such as Bawtry on the River **Idle**. In the centuries before modern road construction, all rivers were used by boats; with their cargoes they sailed as far upstream as they could. In the eighteenth century many canals were built, almost all linked into a major river and so expanded the waterways system still further. Many rivers were also improved to increase water depths with weirs and locks, thereby allowing larger boats to use them. The Trent itself is a good example.

Restoration

Today other transport systems have taken most of the trade from the waterways and, as a result, some canals are now derelict. However, this age of leisure has recognised the potential they hold and many restoration schemes are under way, with more planned for the future. Almost all the work is started by local canal societies: volunteers who give their time freely and are sometimes assisted by the Waterways Recovery Group. If you like getting muddy, join the WRG! Local councils and government financial grants expand the project and eventually a canal is restored to its past splendour. Sections of the **Chesterfield Canal** and the **Grantham Canal** are fine examples of what can be achieved.

Trip-boat John Varley in Tapton Lock, Chesterfield

A towpath designated as a long-distance footpath

Towpaths

The towpaths are a lucky accident of history. Originally built for the horses to tow the boats, they now form a level and easy path alongside most of the waterways mentioned in this book. Standards of surface and width do differ, as maintenance is an ongoing task, but the great majority of towpaths are easy-going. Access for pushchairs and disabled visitors is being improved, as on the **Grantham Canal**. Towpaths are often incorporated into officially signposted walks such as the Cuckoo Way along the **Chesterfield Canal**. Circular walks and cycle routes are covered in booklets for the The Trent Valley Way.

Tidal Rivers

The major rivers of the system are open to the sea, and are therefore, tidal up to the first lock. In certain conditions the incoming tide on the final fifty miles of the Trent can form a bore, like the more famous example the Severn Bore. On the **Trent** it is called the Aegre (pronounced 'ā-ger'). The River **Witham** is tidal between Boston and the Wash.

Small booklets of tide tables can be purchased (see page 209) and these are useful for estimating when vessels may be seen on the rivers and at the locks. Standing at somewhere like **Keadby** on the Trent, it is fascinating to see a major river suddenly start flowing in the opposite direction. The flood risk is always at its greatest when astronomical influences combine to create excessively high tides, and this tidal flow goes into rivers swollen with exceptional amounts of fresh water after prolonged heavy rainfall.

What Can Be Seen

The waterways have many features that tell of their past and present use, some less obvious than others. Stop-plank grooves for instance, are found at narrow sections of canals, often under bridges, they consist of a vertical groove cut into each bank. If a section of canal needs to be drained, for maintenance or to deal with an emergency, then planks are slotted into the grooves to form a dam, thus allowing work to be carried out.

Rope-grooves

Milepost on the Grantham Canal

Also found are winding holes. These are widened sections where vessels can turn round—an important feature if you have a 70ft narrowboat on a narrow canal.

Milestones or posts once lined almost all waterways, necessary because the canal companies charged boatmen tolls per mile. Few original examples survive, but replacements are being installed by canal societies, often in the distinctive style of each waterway—as on the **Grantham Canal**.

Locks

Locks make it possible for boats to rise or fall to a different level on a waterway. They are used to carry the canal channel across hills and down into valleys; on rivers to bypass weirs; and at junctions to allow craft to pass between waterways of differing heights. Most of the locks on, or joining the major rivers, are mechanised and have lock-keepers, especially if tidal waters are involved, but the great majority of locks throughout the system, especially on the canals, are manually operated by boat crews. Lock sizes differ: those on the **Trent** have very large chambers and can accommodate sizeable commercial craft, or a gaggle of small private boats at one time. On the canals, the majority are of two standard widths: narrow locks seven feet wide to take one narrowboat; wide locks fifteen feet across that can take two narrowboats side by side. These are only generalisations, as 200 years of maintenance have created many anomalies.

The most distinctive aspect of manual canal locks is the long balance beams on the gates. Because of the extremely heavy weight of the gates, they can only be moved manually by the leverage supplied by pushing on the long beams. The sluices to let the water in and out, usually called paddles, are operated by winding a steel 'L'-shaped tool called a windlass. Some waterways, especially those in Yorkshire, have different names for the sluice gear and unusual operating systems, but one of the delights of the waterways is finding such varieties. Another type of lock, usually found on rivers, is the guillotine—a graphic name as they have gates that go up and down.

When locks are grouped together along a canal they are known as a 'flight'. And if they are so close together that there is no separate canal between them—that is, boats go straight out of one lock and into another —they are known as a 'staircase flight'. Sometimes staircase flights have side-ponds next to them, small extra reservoirs that help to supply the large amount of water needed to operate such locks. The greatest flights of locks, including staircases, in this area are on the **Chesterfield Canal** but have yet to be restored to navigable condition.

Boats rising to a higher level in locks

Where a canal meets a tidal river, the lock often has two pairs of gates, for example at **Keadby** and **Torksey**. The chevron-shape of closed lock gates always points towards the waterway with the higher water level (A), but with a tidal river this is variable and occasionally the river will be higher than the canal. When that happens the second set of gates (B) is used.

All locks are effectively a dam across a canal or river, therefore, an escape route must be included for the flowing water. On rivers this is a weir, either by the side of the lock or not far away, on canals each lock has a by-wash, a channel down which excess water flows, re-entering the canal near the lower level gates. By-washes are a vital, but often unobtrusive feature, sometimes they even go under nearby buildings.

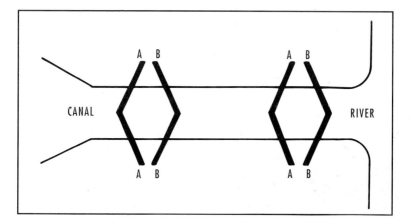

Bridges

There is an endless assortment of bridges, all of which are more interesting, and often more beautiful, when viewed from the bankside rather than from above. Disdainful motorways soar on simple concrete viaducts and railways cross on structures that display the incredible skills of nineteenth-century bricklayers. The humpback bridges common on quiet country roads are often over the oldest canals, their curved lines a delight to the eye. Where the towpath changes from one bank to the other it may be at a special crossing called a turnover bridge, ingeniously designed to allow a boat-horse to move to the opposite bank without the towrope needing to be unhitched from its boat. Some low bridges lift, others swing, to allow boats through, perhaps bearing traffic lights to halt traffic while doing so. The **Stainforth & Keadby Canal** has road lift-bridges, power driven via control boxes operated by boat crews, and a sliding railway bridge.

Roads lift on the New Junction Canal. . .

. . . and swing on the Stainforth & Keadby Canal

Bridges on older canals often bear rope-grooves, cuts made by boat towropes rubbing against the corners of the brick or stonework. Over the years the canal companies tried many solutions to stop the damage—wooden posts that could easily be replaced were installed by bridges to take the wear and tear; a longer-lasting solution was a metal roller to do the same job, turning as a rope dragged past to minimise much of the damaging friction. Few rollers remain, but there is a lovely example on the **Nottingham & Beeston Canal**, though it doesn't turn any more.

Footbridges form a class too wide to simplify. Great numbers are at locks where boat crews have to operate the paddles on both sides; others are in town and city centres; some are on rural rights of way; still more give access to buildings.

Many bridges are numbered in sequence along a waterway, these give visitors a useful reference point and are marked in the handy guidebooks that are available for some canals.

Tunnels

Canal tunnels are old, usually 200 years or more. They were built as a way of taking a canal from one valley to another without using locks to climb all the way up and down a dividing ridge of hills. The construction of each of the longer types was an engineering triumph of the age—expensive in time, money, toil, and sometimes lives. To make such an effort worthwhile the hills crossed had to be quite substantial and, therefore, tunnels are mainly found in Derbyshire and Yorkshire. They differ in length; when it was built the **Cromford Canal** had four tunnels, ranging from the Buckland (32 yards) to the Butterley (2,978 yards).

To save costs, long tunnels were made just wide and high enough to take a boat. Often a towpath was not included and the horses walked over the summit of the hill to meet their boats at the other end. Without the horses the boats had to be propelled by men laying on their backs and pushing their legs against the tunnel wall or roof, a tedious and strenuous system known as 'legging'. Many of the long tunnels are now closed, their restoration creating expensive problems, but finding their bricked-up portals is a fascinating pastime. Some of the shorter ones, for example the 42-yard Gregory on the **Cromford Canal**, have a towpath, and walking through is a murky experience.

Aqueducts

The alternative to a tunnel through a hill, is an aqueduct carrying a canal across whatever may be in a valley—river, road or railway. Like the tunnels they differ in size: some cross small streams and are hardly noticeable, others are magnificent structures. The small types can be found on almost every canal, but the large aqueducts are again in hilly Derbyshire and Yorkshire—the one carrying the **Cromford Canal** over the River Derwent is a fine example. Often built of stone, the early styles are broad and squat to bear the heavy weight of clay and fillings to make the channel watertight. Later aqueducts are more slender structures as the water is contained in an iron trough.

Buildings

There are many buildings that are reminders of the past, a significant number of which still serve today's boaters: old warehouses of all sizes, the 'straddle' variety designed to allow boats to float under the building for loading; tall industrial buildings; and warehouses with doors on each floor opening out onto the waterway, the remains of the pulleys and cranes that moved the cargoes between those doorways and the boats moored below still visible. Examples of lock-keepers' houses, wharf offices, stables and blacksmiths' shops for the boat-horses, old pubs, maintenance sheds, and water mills have all survived. Canal company office buildings are rare but the **Sleaford Navigation** has one, in addition to a water mill under restoration at the first lock.

Houses that were built for lock-keepers, and are no longer required, are much-sought-after private homes. Warehouses have been altered into restaurants, stables into post offices, and mills into snooker halls. Some of the older waterside pubs are the survivors of those that supplied food and beds for boatmen, and stables for their horses. Pub names often tell of past usage—such as the Packet Inn where villagers used to catch the packet, or public transport boat, to a nearby market town. Others include The Ship, The Navigation, The Brick & Tile (boat cargoes), The Old Silk Mill and The Ferry Inn.

Boats

Such is the fascination of boats that a separate chapter has been allocated to their description (see page 191). A greater variety of craft can be seen in this area than anywhere else in the country: narrowboats; cruisers; skiffs; barges; sea-going ships; yachts; converted lifeboats; keels; rowing-eights; gin-palaces; canoes; house-boats; trip-boats; hotel-boats; hire-boats and trail-boats.

Provided for their use are slipways, wharves, cranes, boat-houses, mooring pontoons, bollards and boatyards.

Warehouse with doors where goods were lowered to and from boats moored below, Nottingham

Toll-collector's hut, now a summer-house, Slea Navigation

Old Canal Company offices, Sleaford

Wildlife

The waterways are an important and rich habitat for many creatures and plants. A wide variety of wildlife is encouraged by the differing patterns of water flow. The canals provide fresh water that is slow moving and of moderate depth. As a result, there is a greater range of daily and annual water temperatures, the bottom deposits remaining relatively undisturbed. Rivers, on the other hand, differ widely in flow, depth and seasonal variations—and in tidal sections salt water is mixed with fresh. Neighbouring fields, especially those flooded in the winter, also supply a different environment.

Birds such as coots, moorhens, grebes and swans can be seen on many waterways, some of them often on the banks and in surrounding fields. In the winter cormorants are widespread on estuaries and nearby inland waters, usually perched on man-made structures. In the summer swallows and martins swoop low over the surface catching insects. The largest bird commonly seen is the heron—during the day standing at the water's edge, flapping away at the last minute when disturbed. But never forgotten is seeing an eye-catching bright flash of intense blue, flying at up to 25mph low to the water—a kingfisher. Happily these exotic-looking birds are not rare and can be seen on town waterways as well as in the country, but you've got to be quick!

Rabbits, hares, foxes and squirrels are common in waterside fields; stoats and weasels hunt in towpath hedges. The first sign of a water vole is often the ripples made as it swims from bank to bank. Newts and frogs like damp, dark vegetation near the water, and bats emerge soon after sunset to hunt for insects.

In June and July dragonflies flit about. On the water's surface there are specialist insects such as pond-skaters, whirligig beetles and waterboatmen.

There are hundreds of different flowering plants, most of which are best seen between June and September. Some like damp conditions near, but out of, the water, others have their roots in the water's edge, and many settle for halfway depth.

The speed of flow, depth, oxygen content and amount of water-weed all define the types of fish that will thrive in each waterway. It is quite common for one species to be virtually absent from the main river, for example the **Witham**, but abundant in tributaries such as the **Slea** and the **Bain** because the conditions suit it better. The exception is the eel, an incredible fish that can live in any water. Bream, carp, chub, perch, pike, roach and tench are all present in this area.

Angling
There is top-class angling on many of the waterways in the area, especially the rivers Trent and Witham. On almost every stretch angling is organised by various societies and clubs, many based in Yorkshire cities and towns. The regulations on day tickets, licences and fees are available from the clubs—see page 205.

Cycling
A permit is required to ride on towpaths maintained by British Waterways. Available from the BW office listed at the end of each chapter, the permits are free and must be displayed on a cycle. BW will also provide information on the towpaths suitable for cycling. A useful leaflet is Cycling by Train, available from rail stations. Cycles are not allowed on the Sheffield Supertram system.

Maintenance

Water Supplies
The water supply is an aspect of canals that is overlooked by many visitors. Rivers, as natural features, look after themselves to a great degree, but canals are man-made and rely on water being specifically channelled in and out of them.

Every time a lock is used it passes thousands of gallons of water to the lower level of a canal, so a supply is always required at the canal's highest level to replace it. These inflows are called feeders and they bring water diverted from nearby rivers, or collected in reservoirs higher in the hills. The amount of water required depends on the terrain—the steeper the hills, the more locks, the more water needed. The **Erewash Canal** uses water from its name river, the **Horncastle Canal** from the Bain; the **Cromford**, **Grantham** and **Chesterfield Canals** are supplied by rivers and reservoirs.

Much effort and maintenance is required to keep the system operational so wasting water on a canal is a serious misdemeanour. Therefore boaters have rules for using locks, an etiquette designed to use as little water as possible.

As water is always passing down a canal, it is of equal importance to have an outlet when it reaches the lowest level; back into the nearest river—usually the river the canal was built to link with anyway. Between the summit and the lowest level, canals also have spillways, channels where excess water, perhaps from heavy rainfall, can safely flow away to a river.

Flood Defences

Although the waterways are now primarily used for leisure, every water-course, no matter how insignificant, also has a role in the vital task of draining the land. Over many years, elaborate systems of flood defence have been installed and these are now the responsibility of the National Rivers Authority (NRA). Even so, prolonged torrential rain still causes problems, and will probably always do so. Controlling nature is an expensive and ultimately impossible aim. The **Trent** has major flood prevention weirs and controls at Nottingham, and further downstream floodbanks defend millions of acres of low-lying farmland. The River **Idle** drains a vast area of Nottinghamshire and powerful sluices keep the tide on the Trent out. The **Witham**, flowing through flat Lincolnshire countryside, is also a major flood-control river, its own banks dotted with numerous sluices and outlets through which flows the water from an intricate network of ditches and dykes.

Who Looks After it All?

Today the two main national authorities are British Waterways (BW), and the National Rivers Authority (NRA). This is a new dual respon-sibility, the latest in centuries of administrative evolution on the water-ways, and still a candidate for future change. The offices and yards of both organisations can be seen throughout the national waterways sys-tem, their duties sometimes overlapping. There are often divided obliga-tions on rivers with one body looking after navigation—carrying out the installation and maintenance of all the facilities needed by boaters, including locks—and another controlling all the other aspects of the waterway.

If major repairs are needed, it is sometimes necessary to close a water-way to boats. Unless an emergency occurs, such projects are scheduled for the winter, when there are fewer craft about, and the date and duration of the stoppage is published in advance in the waterways' magazines.

The NRA and BW have twenty-four-hour emergency telephone numbers on which the public can report waterway problems or emergencies. (See page 208.)

British Waterways is a nationalised industry, part-funded by the gov-ernment. It owns, operates and maintains the majority of the canal sys-tem —nationally over 2,000 miles of waterways two centuries old. To look after the canals BW has a fleet of workboats; tugs, floating cranes and dredgers, which can be seen around the system. BW is also the navigation authority on many rivers, some 23,000 pleasure craft are licensed, and commercial vessels move four million tonnes of freight

British Waterways maintenance staff working on the Aire & Calder Navigation

British Waterways visitor information sign

each year. Angling rights are controlled, towpaths are mown, signs erected, and leaflets published.

At strategic points throughout the system BW has installed facilities for the use of boat crews, these are known as 'sanitary stations', the simplest consisting of toilets and a drinking water supply. The latest styles also have showers and sometimes laundries. Access is gained by a special Yale key—its twee official name is the 'Watermate'—that boaters buy from BW, a useful item in this area where it also unlocks gates to mooring pontoons and the control-panels of mechanised locks and lift-bridges.

BW has had many names since its creation in 1947, and many people and signs still refer to its last identity, BWB (British Waterways Board).

The **National Rivers Authority** was established in 1989, it has a wide range of legal responsibilities. These include water pollution control, flood and sea defences, conservation of water resources, environmental improvements, fisheries, recreation and navigation. A great deal of the NRA's time is spent monitoring water standards, wildlife and plants so that problems can be located and resolved. It has an interest in the canals, even if they are controlled by BW, because the water in them is often supplied from, and returned to, NRA rivers.

Glossary of Terms

Aegre. A large wave on the River Trent that sometimes accompanies the incoming tide. Similar to the tidal bore on the River Severn.

Balance beams. The long beams on manually-operated lock gates. The length gives the leverage necessary to push open a heavy gate.

Barge. A general term for modern cargo carrying river/canal craft, operated by commercial companies.

Beam. The width of a boat.

Bollard. Short metal posts for boat ropes to be tied to. Usually at locks and wharves.

Brindley, James. Engineer who built many canals in the 1760s and '70s.

BW, BWB. British Waterways; used to be British Waterways Board.

BW key. A special Yale key used by boaters to operate powered locks and lift/swing-bridges, open gates, and to gain access to sanitary facilities and emergency telephones. Also known as a Watermate.

By-wash. A channel down which excess water can flow to bypass a canal lock.

Canal societies. Voluntary groups who promote the use and/or restoration of a particular canal.

Canalware. The brightly painted cans, plant-pots, utensils, etc. seen on narrowboats. Traditional designs.

Cut. A canal. Also on a river; an artificial section with a lock(s) built to bypass a weir or shallows.

Feeders. Channels along which the water supply to a canal is fed.

Flight. A series of locks very close together.

Flood-gates, flood-lock. Barriers on a river that are closed to protect lock-cuts if water levels rise excessively. In normal conditions these gates and locks are left open.

Gongoozler. Someone who stands and watches boats, usually at locks.

Guillotine gate. A lock gate that goes vertically up and down, rather than swinging open.

Handspike. A length of wood used to open lock sluices. Calder & Hebble Navigation only.

Head of navigation. The furthest point along a canal or river that can be reached by boat.

Hotel-boats. Usually two narrowboats working together, with crews. Floating hotels for those who wish to cruise the waterways without doing the boat-handling themselves.

IWA. Inland Waterways Association. A national group with local branches. Promotes waterway interests.

Jessop, William. Famous waterways engineer in the 1790s.

Keels. The barges which carried cargoes on waterways in this area. Originally sail-driven, later with engines.

Legging. The old method of moving non-engine-powered boats through tunnels when there was no towpath for the horse. Boatmen lay on their backs and 'walked' their legs along the wall or roof of the tunnel, thereby pushing the boat along.

Lengthsman. Responsible for the maintenance of a specific length of canal.

Lock, narrow/wide. Narrow locks are seven feet wide and narrowboats are designed to fit into them. Wide locks are approximately fifteen feet wide and can be used by two narrowboats side by side, or by large river craft. The terms 'wide' and 'narrow' canals refer to their lock sizes. In this area only the Chesterfield Canal west of Retford has narrow locks.

Lock, four sets of gates. Usually at the junction of a canal and a tidal river, e.g. Torksey, Keadby. See page 15 for description and diagram.

Lock-cut. On a river, a short section of canal with one or more locks that allows boats to bypass an obstruction, usually a weir.

Lock flight. A series of locks very close together.

Longboat. Used by the Vikings. An incorrect name for a narrowboat.

Narrowboat. A boat six feet ten inches wide (beam), designed for narrow canals and locks. Can be any length up to 70ft. They are not longboats, they are not barges.

Narrow canal, Narrow locks. See Locks, narrow/wide.Navigation. A river that has been improved for boat usage by the creation of cuts (canal sections) and locks to bypass weirs or shallows.

Neap tides. See Tides.

NRA. National Rivers Authority.

Packet-boat. Old public passenger transport system. Regular service boats that used to call at towns, villages and pubs, operated to a timetable.

Paddles, paddle-gear. The sluices that can be opened and closed to let water into and out of locks.

Pound. A level length of canal between two locks. Can be yards or miles long.

Puddle. The saturated mud used to create a water-tight seal on the bottom and sides of canals.

Pulley Stones. Stones with a pulley on top to help horse-towed boats around tight bends. Barnsley Canal only.

Reach. A length of river, often between bends.

Rope-marks, rope-grooves. Cuts caused by the rubbing of boat tow-ropes many years ago. Often on bridge edges.

Roving bridge. See Turnover bridge.

Side-pond. Extra reservoirs of water by the side of large flights of locks. In this area, only on the Norwood flight of the Chesterfield Canal.

Slipway. A slope down which boats can be launched into the water, or pulled out.

Spring tides. See Tides.

Staircase locks. Two or more locks with no intervening canal between them. In this area, only on the Chesterfield Canal.

Stop-lock. At the junction of two canals, the official point where one starts and the other ends. The lock usually has a rise/fall of only a few inches.

Stop-plank grooves. Vertical grooves in both banks of a canal, often under bridges. Planks can be slipped into them to form a dam across the canal if a section has to be drained for repairs.

Summit pound. The highest section of a canal.

Tidal lock. The first lock upstream from the mouth of a tidal river. Therefore the limit of the tide's influence on the river.

Tides (neap, spring). Tide heights go in a cycle of 14–16 days, influenced by the moon and sun. Within that cycle, neap tides have the smallest range of heights between low water and high water. Spring tides— not a reference to a yearly season—have the greatest range, that is they rise higher and fall lower.

Spring tide	High water level	---
Neap tide	High water level	—————————————————
Neap tide	Low water level	—————————————————
Spring tide	Low water level	---

Within the 14–16-day cycle the high-water levels will gradually increase and reach a peak with the spring tides. Then the high-water marks will gradually subside on each tide, until reaching the bottom of the cycle with neap tides. However, in a river the tidal low-water mark is mainly irrelevant because there is always a supply of freshwater flowing down. See page 209 for tide table availability.

Tom Puddings. A system of separate containers, joined together and pulled by a tug. Usually carried coal. Each container tipped up by a hoist to shoot the coal into a ship. Operated on the Aire & Calder Navigation for many years until 1986.

Turnover bridge. Where a towpath changes from one bank to the other.

Watermate. See BW key.

Water supply. The streams, rivers, reservoirs that supply water to a canal.

Wharfinger. An old term for an official in charge of a wharf; checking cargoes, security, charging fees, organising boats, etc.

Wide canal, wide locks. See Locks, narrow/wide.

Winding hole. A wide section of a narrow waterway where lengthy boats can be turned.

Windlass. An L-shaped implement used to open and close lock sluices.

WRG. Waterways Recovery Group. National voluntary group involved in canal restoration.

The Cromford Canal

Unnavigable; 14.5 miles long
7 wide locks and 3 narrow tunnels remain
OS map: Landranger sheets 119, 120, 129

THE first mile of the Cromford Canal from Cromford Wharf to Leawood *is a gem, a marvellous example of the wide variety of attractions that draw people to inland waterways. It's one of my favourites, an outing that never disappoints because no matter how many times I go I always discover something missed before. The majority of visitors come for a quiet towpath walk through Derbyshire's beautiful Peak District, others enjoy canoeing, watching the waterbirds, or picnicking at the tables provided. For people interested in canals in their own right, there is a wonderful collection of features to see and study: old wharf buildings, a notable aqueduct over the River Derwent, a canal and railway transhipment wharf— and a fine pumphouse with a working steam-powered beam-engine.*

With such attractions it's easy to forget the rest of the route and the fact that the Cromford is not only a canal of the Peak District—east of Ripley it passes through the coal-ravaged areas near Ironville. Of course, one part of the canal has all the visitors, the other hardly any, but both sections are worth exploring if you are interested in a complete picture of this waterway.

Abandoned as a navigable canal in 1944, the Cromford is in a variety of conditions along its 14.5 miles. In the Peak District the western end provides a level towpath along the delightful Derwent valley, with rail stations at Cromford, Whatstandwell and Ambergate providing return transport to a starting point. The towpath also links with the popular High Peak Trail.

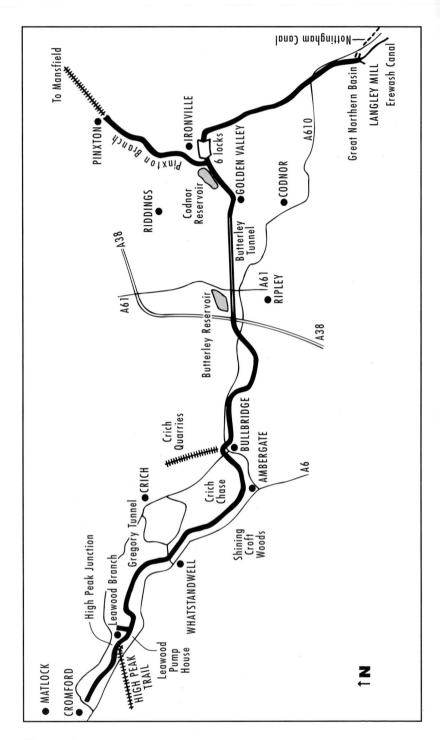

The five-mile section from Cromford to Ambergate is owned by the local council and maintained as an amenity for visitors to enjoy. Within that length, Whatstandwell to Ambergate is managed as a nature reserve by the Derbyshire Wildlife Trust.

At Ambergate the canal turns due east into the valley of the River Amber, then, via Butterley Tunnel, it enters the River Erewash's valley for the final descent from the hills. The eastern terminus is a junction with two other canals at Langley Mill, the Nottingham and the Erewash providing links to the River Trent and the national waterways network.

Along the route is a major canal tunnel: the Butterley at nearly 3,000 yards was one of the longest in the country. A major feat of engineering for the 1790s, the tunnel lasted for 100 years until mining subsidence finally caused its closure in 1900. The eastern portal can still be seen near Golden Valley, north of Ripley.

Two of the canal's reservoirs are now used for public leisure: Butterley for sailing, Codnor Park for walking and fishing. The towpath, alongside abandoned locks, is used by local people near Ironville and at Langley Mill, the last lock of the Cromford has been restored and is now used to give access to moorings for boats cruising the Erewash Canal.

The wharf at Cromford

THE WESTERN terminus of the canal is at Cromford Wharf; just off the A6 south of Matlock Bath and clearly indicated by brown 'tourist attraction' road signs. There is a large car park, toilets, and picnic tables on the grassy canal bank.

A sign of the past, Cromford Wharf

Most of what was the wharf's open storage area is now the car park but a lovely collection of old buildings still huddle round the last yards of the canal: stables and a wharfinger's office of mellow stone with grey slate roofs, warehouses with wooden canopies to protect boat cargoes from the weather, and everywhere small reminders of working days such as mooring rings, crane remains, road wagon unloading bays, and rope marks. The open aspect of the wharf is misleading as the whole area was originally encircled by a massive stone wall to prevent theft of cargoes, but the modern car park entrance has cut through the wall and some buildings on the far side have been demolished. It's worth taking the time to explore and to try to imagine the activity of past centuries.

It's not a coincidence that the historic Arkwright Mill is just across the road from the wharf. In the 1790s the roads were bad, the railways still in the future, and Sir Richard Arkwright needed canal transport to expand the trade of his already phenomenally successful cotton mill. Sir Richard was a keen promoter of the scheme to build the canal and even agreed that the canal company could build the wharf on what was then the garden of his home, Rock House, still high above on the adjacent stone cliff.

The larger arm of the wharf was for incoming traffic with ground areas reserved for the storage of coal, timber and other goods, the raw cotton taken direct to the mill across the road. Outgoing goods went from the arm of the wharf nearest to the stone cliff; mainly limestone that was heaped outside on the wharfside, and processed cotton yarn from the Arkwright Mill. At the end of this arm a feeder stream delivers the canal's initial supply of water, which has come under the road from the cotton mills where it used to drive the waterwheels—another

CROMFORD WHARF

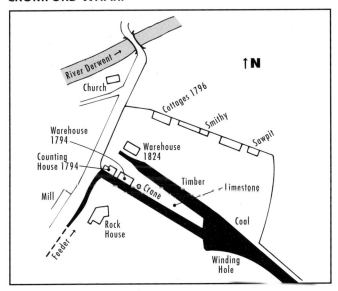

example of Sir Richard Arkwright's involvement in the building of the canal. Moored on the feeder during my last visit was an old boat that used to give horse-drawn public trips here, a service now sadly lacking, although it may be restored in the future.

At the end of the stone-lined wharf, where the canal proper starts, there is a wider section where the lengthy narrowboats could turn. The other features that make this section of the Cromford Canal so interesting are one mile from here along the towpath, at High Peak Junction and Leawood.[1]

The towpath from the wharf is a popular route; a level walk in the Peak District is always a great attraction. The path is wide, surfaced, well drained, tree-lined, and accompanied by a canal full of water and, on summer weekends, canoeists.[2] In all hilly areas, transport routes use the river valleys whenever possible—it's cheaper to use the line of least resistance—and for its first six miles the canal follows the River Derwent, sidling alongside the railway and road as they all share the valley. It may sound as if this would spoil the atmosphere of the canal, but each transport system is on a different level and somehow they all co-exist without friction—on the far bank the A6 is hidden, and quietened,

1. *If not wishing to walk, there is a car park on the Cromford-to-Lea road from where a footbridge gives direct access to the canal at High Peak Junction.*
2. *Canoeing with permission only. Contact the Visitor Centres at High Peak Junction or Middleton Top.*

by a wooded hillside, and the trains are quiet, fast and short and make little impact on the canal scene.

At the bottom of the valley silvery glimpses of the Derwent can be seen through the trees as it rushes along on its way to meet the Trent near Shardlow. The canal's height above the river is a testament to the skill of its builders: they managed to construct a canal on one level all the way from Cromford to Ironville—even if it did need two aqueducts and four tunnels to do it. To build anything level for 11.5 miles in the Peak District is a great achievement, even by today's standards.

About a mile from Cromford a gentle sweep to the right brings the canal to High Peak Junction, a swing-bridge giving access to the old workshop buildings of the Cromford & High Peak Railway, closed in 1967, its track line converted into the popular High Peak Trail. At busy times in the summer the workshops are open to the public and contain an information centre, a museum and toilets. Outside are picnic tables by the canal and, the almost mandatory ducks.

The railway was a means of taking goods across the Pennines to Whaley Bridge situated on the Peak Forest Canal, thereby giving access to customers in Lancashire, Manchester and Liverpool. It opened in 1831 and was not a railway in today's conventional sense—the wagons were pulled up the steep gradients by horses, later static engines at the top of each slope took over. It was very profitable and at High Peak Junction goods were transhipped between the boats and the railway wagons. The site where the goods were transferred is further along where an old warehouse is on the edge of the canal. Boats came alongside for loading and unloading, some goods were stored in the warehouse, others were loaded straight onto railway wagons lined up under the canopy at the far end, the tracks running through the building. The warehouse is now used as classrooms and accommodation for school study groups.

A little distance along the canal from High Peak Junction, on the towpath side, is Leawood pumphouse, its tall chimney towering over one of the finest examples of canal architecture to be found. The decorative finish achieved by contrasting smooth and rough stone surfaces is a testament to the skill of the masons that built it. Inside is a magnificent steam-powered beam engine, lovingly restored and still doing the job for which it was installed in 1849. In the 1840s the canal's water source at Cromford Wharf began to decline and this engine was placed here to pump another supply up from the Derwent. One cycle of the engine sucks water from the river through a 150-yard tunnel to a reservoir under the pumphouse, the beam then falls to lift four tons of water thirty feet into the canal. The engine can be seen working on published weekends in the summer: the pumphouse becomes a cathedral of hissing

Leawood Pumphouse

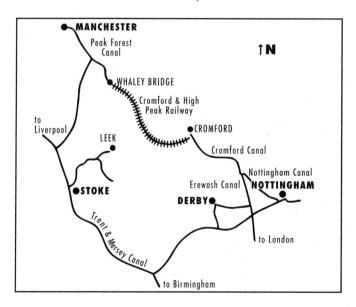

35

steam with boiler-suited 'priests' and respectful worshippers, the object of their devotion a green-painted engine of mesmerising power.[3]

The pumphouse is at the end of Leawood (Wigwell) Aqueduct where the canal crosses the Derwent to run along the other side of the valley. From the stone-walled towpath the river can be seen noisily rushing underneath, but the problem with appreciating aqueducts is that when walking over them very little can be seen of the structure below. This example has three arches, the centre one with a span of eighty feet across the river, but from above nothing can be seen of the challenge overcome by its eighteenth-century builders. It is possible to reach the river to view the aqueduct—the path is at the Cromford end, on the far side via the footbridge over the canal. A path leads down through the trees to the edge of the Derwent, and the aqueduct can be seen in all its glory—including the date 1792 over the central span.

At the end of the aqueduct is the entrance to the 550-yard Leawood Branch, otherwise known as the Nightingale Arm because it was built in 1802 to bring canal transport to Peter Nightingale's lead works at Lea Bridge. A ruined lengthman's cottage is in the trees by the junction and it is possible to walk along the canal arm—a pleasant detour high on the bank alongside the Derwent, a footbridge over the railway, where the canal used to cross on an aqueduct, and, outside Wharf Cottage, the terminus, marked by a paved area with the metal circle of a crane base. This is another of the quiet places that played a part in the Industrial Revolution and now rest forgotten by all except those who love our canals.

On the main line of the canal the towpath changes sides via a footbridge at the end of the aqueduct. From now on the canal still holds water, but it may be lower in the channel depending on the supply available. However, the towpath is still good and the atmosphere quieter, the majority of people only walking as far as Leawood. A more natural environment encourages waterbirds and a wide variety is evident along here—I've seen a kingfisher swooping along just above the water's surface, and a dumpy little dabchick diving beneath overhanging bushes. In this rural setting there is something of the feel of an urban canal in the way today's century busily speeds along its road, totally unaware of you in a nearby earlier world.

The canal is hidden on a tree-clad hillside, the land beyond the towpath dropping away to the valley floor where the road and the river now take a more distant route. The railway, of which little has been seen or heard for some time, makes a dramatic return as the canal crosses it on another aqueduct. This example is more mundane than the one

3. *Details of working days from Matlock Tourist Information or the Visitor Centre at Middleton Top.*

over the Derwent, the canal's water contained in a plain iron trough with a balustrade edging the towpath. Only a few yards away the railway tracks disappear into the awful blackness of a tunnel—generating a primaeval compulsion to stop and wait for 'something' to come out of the hellish cave.

For a distance the canal has the hillside to itself, a quiet, secluded, forested path—and still level. Traffic noise is muted and distant, only noticeable if listened for. Shallow bends make the walk interesting and one to the left reveals Gregory's Tunnel, this time on the canal not the railway. The stonework, shrouded in greenery in the summer, rises high over the entrance and the towpath disappears into the tunnel—but it's only 76 yards long. Even so, the light from both portals doesn't quite illuminate the whole length but there is no danger of stumbling from the path as it has a post-and-rail fence along the edge. At the entrance there's a stop-plank groove in the stonework, important as there are no locks here to protect a leaking canal. Past the tunnel the water may be shallow, sometimes choked with reeds, and in summer the towpath can become overgrown but it remains passable.

Between Whatstandwell and Ambergate the banks are thickly wooded; the old hunting forest of Crich Chase on the far side, the splendidly named Shining Cliff Woods on the near side. Not that the old boatmen could enjoy this area at leisure; to stop them poaching, and to placate the landowners, the canal company had a bye-law banning boats from stopping in Crich Chase or any other wood or coppice. In the spring the towpath is lined with flowers—violets, anemones, yellow archangel. On the damper soil of the upper banks the meadowsweet's masses of small cream flowers dominate from July onwards. This stretch of the canal is managed by the Derbyshire Wildlife Trust, and 'managed' is the correct word, as a few water plants can become invasive and would oust many others if not controlled. Most summers the Trust hand-clears them from the waterway although some are allowed to remain as a habitat for less common insects.

Unfortunately, this section of the canal ends at Ambergate, the line obliterated by a huge gas pipeline complex. Between here and Golden Valley bits and pieces of the Cromford Canal have survived and searching for them is like a treasure hunt. Clues such as the name of the Canal Inn at Bullbridge lead to the discovery of the towpath, here a footpath, emerging from the side of Stevenson's dye-works. On the other side of the road, near the pub, is a house with a few yards of water-filled canal as a feature in the garden, on the towpath is a rusty old boundary post of the Midland Railway, past owner of the canal.[4]

4. *On the Crich road from the A610 at Bullbridge.*

Midland Railway boundary post, Ambergate

The canal used to pass over the River Amber, the railway and the A610 on the Bullbridge Aqueduct, but it was blown up in 1968 to make the road wider. It can be found where the western end of the aqueduct banking meets the A610; there is an old chapel nearby and terraced houses with the old road in front, the towpath regained via a gateway marked with the Cromford Canal towpath logo.

At the end of the lower car park of The Excavator pub is a gem of a find—Buckland Hollow Tunnel has been here for two centuries and it's still in perfect condition. The design is the same as Gregory's Tunnel but it's less than half the length, only 33 yards. There's a towpath through, although the bed of the canal has been filled in. It's a quiet, deserted, hidden, secret place.[5]

From here the canal veered sharply to the right, now the route to the pub's upper car park, and the line can be picked up beyond that car park where its continuation is marked by towpath badges. Not far from here the canal disappeared into Butterley Tunnel, almost 3,000 yards of darkness. Above it is Butterley Reservoir, alongside the A61 north of

5. *East of Bullbridge at the junction of the A610 and B6013.*

38

Ripley, built to supply water to the canal. The eastern portal of the great tunnel can be found at Golden Valley, via a good path at the side of the Newlands Inn. In the summer it is easy to miss the tunnel entrance as it's sometimes hidden and overgrown by bushes and plants, the main clue being the sound of water flowing down a feeder by the portal. A visit in the winter or early spring, when the vegetation has died down, usually reveals the tunnel's black maw.

Butterley tunnel has done more than pass through a hill: it has brought the canal to the coal-rich Erewash valley. Today open-cast mining is still taking place and the area wears a tired air of resignation, endless abuse the cost of its mineral treasure. But it should be remembered that the coal of this area was the main impetus for the construction of the canal; without the sacrifice of the Erewash valley there would not be a picturesque man-made waterway at Cromford.

The canal's Codnor Park Reservoir is near Golden Valley, its waters now used for fishing, its banks topped by an encircling path. The air is fresh and breezy and at the eastern end a footbridge, adjacent to the car park, crosses over the old canal and gives access to the towpath and six locks. The isolated stone bridge at the end of the reservoir took the towpath over the 2.5 mile Pinxton branch, built to reach cargoes of coal, pottery and perishable goods. Open-cast mining has obliterated much of the line but the wharf at Pinxton has been restored as a picnic area.[6]

Along the main canal at Ironville the towpath is easy to follow, much of its length used by local people, and six old locks can be seen, one end of a flight of fourteen that took the canal down the valley to Langley Mill. The top lock, not far from the Pinxton bridge, is the canal's first change of level in the 11.5 miles from hilly Cromford. Standing by this lock it hardly seems possible that the surrounding semi-industrial area could be linked by a level route to tourist-festooned Cromford. But it's true, and typical of canals; the wide variety of the areas each may cross often defying a simple description of the waterway.

The size of the locks is interesting because they could take wide boats, but such boats were unable to go much farther along the canal because the tunnels between here and Cromford could only take narrowboats. The reason was construction costs: to build a wide 3,000-yard Butterley Tunnel would have been expensive in time and money, and by reaching Ironville the wide boats already had access to the lucrative coalfields, so the canal owners judged the cost of taking them up to Cromford unnecessary.

6. *Access to the wharf at Pinxton is via Wharf Road and Alexander Terrace, by the railway level crossing.*

The locks are gateless and in various states of decay, their brick-lined verdant chambers allowing the overflow waters from the reservoir to run unhindered. Most of the pounds are reedy, but by a trick of nature one stretch of water was clear on my last visit and it was a delight to see a heron in such an unlikely area. Eventually the canal swings to the south and within half a mile it disappears at the remains of a railway embankment.[7]

Through Stoneyford there is little to be seen but at Langley Mill the final yards, and the last lock, of the Cromford Canal end in a complete contrast—a fully-restored and usually boat-filled Great Northern Basin. Historic circumstance has resulted in the Erewash Canal surviving as a navigable waterway and at its junction with the Cromford the basin has been preserved by local canal enthusiasts. Today the lock and the basin are used as part of the Erewash Canal but they are nevertheless the final representatives of a waterway of only 14.5 miles, but of abundant variety—the Cromford Canal.

7. *Restoration of the locks and downstream to Langley Mill is being investigated.*

Great Northern Basin, Langley Mill

Further Reading

Hadfield, Charles, *The Canals of the East Midlands* (David & Charles). History.

The Cromford Canal: Walking Britain's Heritage (Free leaflet available from the Amber Valley Groundwork Trust, 19 Bridge St, Belper, Derbyshire; Tel: 01773 824588).

Cromford Canal Nature Reserve (Three free leaflets on the birds, plants, and insects. Available from the Derbyshire Wildlife Trust, Elvaston Castle, Derby DE7 3EP; Tel: 01332 756610).

Useful Contacts

British Waterways Manager responsible for the canal. Tel: 0115 946 1017. Office by the side of Trent Lock, Erewash Canal.

Inland Waterways Association Tel: 0115 987 5475.

Visitor Centre, High Peak Junction Tel: 01629 822831.

Visitor Centre, Middleton Top Tel: 01629 823204.

Public Transport

Rail Stations (Nearest)* Cromford, Whatstandwell*, Ambergate*, Langley Mill.

Bus Latest details from 'Busline'. Tel: 01332 292200.

Places to Visit in the Area

Tourist Information Matlock. Tel: 01629 55082.

Arkwright's Cromford Mill, Cromford. Remains of the site of the world's first successful water-powered cotton spinning mill. Free access, guided tours, shops, café. Tel: 01629 824297/823256.

National Tramway Museum, Crich. Rides on vintage trams, exhibitions, special events, museum, shops. Tel: 01773 852565.

Midland Railway Centre, Butterley Station, Ripley. Steam train rides, museum, miniature railway, special events. Tel: 01773 747674/749788; Visitor Information Line: 01773 570140.

Gulliver's Kingdom, Matlock Bath. Children's rides, water features, fantasy lands, etc. Tel: 01629 57100.

Heights of Abraham, Matlock Bath. Cable cars to grounds and caverns on the hills. Tel: 01629 582365.

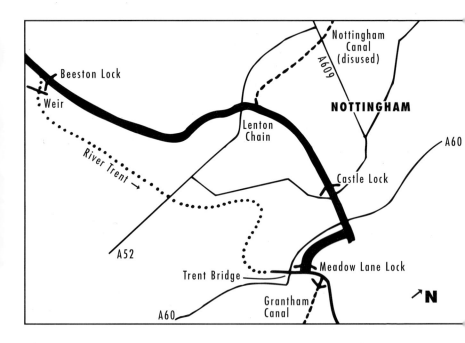

Beeston Lock

Weir

River Trent →

Nottingham Canal (disused)

A609

NOTTINGHAM

Lenton Chain

A60

Castle Lock

A52

Trent Bridge

Meadow Lane Lock

A60

Grantham Canal

N

The Nottingham Canal and Beeston Cut

Navigable for 6 miles, with 3 wide locks
unnavigable for a further 12 miles
OS map: Landranger sheet 129

THE Nottingham & Beeston Canal is navigable and busy: the route that all craft must take to avoid a weir-barred section of the River Trent.

It passes through Nottingham city centre and is a waterway of diverse atmosphere: old industrial buildings and warehouses still looking as they must have done to the working boatmen, others renovated and put to new use, a marina, pleasant open areas in the city centre, prize-winning modern architecture, industrial areas, and Nottingham's ancient castle. At its western end the canal meets the River Trent with a background of open fields and hills, the air fresh and invigorating.

Because of the canal's 'river bypass' nature, and its length of only six miles, the Nottingham & Beeston is often overlooked—walkers on the Trent Valley Way have no need of it and keep to the river's towpath; boaters mentally see it as a part of the Trent Navigation and seldom notice it as a canal in its own right. But that is to miss a great deal.

In addition to the canal's varied route through Nottingham, there are numerous canal features to be seen: a rope-roller, wide locks, turnover bridges, and a lock-house, a waterways junction, a canal museum and a trip-boat.

A GOOD place to start a visit is a few hundred yards from the famous Trent Bridge and near Notts County football ground. Access to the canal is via a stone bridge bearing a blue 'canal towpath' sign, opposite The Greyhound pub on London Road (A60). Unfortunately, the towpath going towards the nearby Trent is not a public right of way, a locked gate bars access to the canal's junction with the river at Meadow Lane lock. However, walking towards the city centre soon compensates for that early disappointment.

The magic of canals in urban districts is that a step onto a towpath is a step away from modern life and its noisy hurrying, its dust and its pressures; that soon becomes evident on the Nottingham & Beeston. The towpath is wide and surfaced, on both sides stone walls rise to the level where the twentieth century operates. Down by the canal is an age apart.

The water is clean—and so it should be, it's only been borrowed from the Trent. A tiny fraction of the river is diverted into the canal at Beeston to flow through six man-made miles until it is released back into the Trent via Meadow Lane Lock. A variety of bridges cross the canal, all types, all sizes, many colours: footbridges of painted wrought iron, Victorian road bridges with sturdy stone piers and fancy iron balustrades, railway viaducts of blue engineering bricks.

London Road continues to run parallel, but the traffic noise soon lessens as the road rises ever higher on an embankment. London Road's local nickname used to be 'Flood Road', as it frequently was! Over the years its embankment has been raised many times and from the towpath can be seen the different layers of stone, brick, and cement of two centuries of improvements.

Quite often traffic is held up on bridges over a city canal and those in the vehicles always seem to gaze down upon you with a blank expression, as if they're looking at another world they cannot recognise. They probably never noticed what was under the bridge before, but there are people down there today—how odd! And you look up at them as if they are uncomprehending tourists. Then the traffic moves on and the two worlds divide once again.

Those motorists will probably never know that just along here boats used to load at 'Sani Wharf'. No sign of it remains today, which may be a blessing. The cargo was 'nightsoil', the old name for the contents of the earth closets of Nottingham's notorious tenement slums. It was obviously obnoxious, but nevertheless it was a valuable cargo and, taken across the Trent and along the Grantham Canal, it was sold to farmers as fertiliser for their fields. I shall leave you to imagine the boatman's working day on this trade. I've always found that knowledge of such cargoes is a good antidote if I'm smitten with blissful dreams and romantic visions of past life on the canals.

One seldom-seen item that has survived on this stretch is a rope-roller

Old warehouses, Nottingham

on one of the stone bridges. It doesn't turn now, but it's a splendid example nevertheless. The usual rope marks made by the boat tow-ropes are clear on the edge of the bridge. Sometimes wooden or iron uprights were placed in front of the stonework to act as rubbing posts, but these needed replacing quite often as the ropes eventually wore grooves in them. A roller was an imaginative solution to a common problem.

Bridges increase in frequency on the approach to the city centre. By now London Road is high on its embankment and traffic noise has faded to a dull murmur. Down by the canal the loudest sound is the cooing of the pigeons that roost on every crevice. There always seems to be a large number of pipes near a city canal; all sizes, colours, shapes. They emerge from walls or buildings and cross the water by disappearing into the ground or running along the bridge tops. One wonders what they all contain, perhaps it's best not to know.

Ahead are the massive girders of a high-level railway viaduct, built in 1899 to carry the trains of the Great Northern Railway to its new Victoria Station. Now isolated and disused, it is still an immense structure and a further example of Victorian confidence. Just before the viaduct is a fine turnover bridge, the stonework now cleaned and restored as part of a scheme to turn the adjacent old railway station into a Museum of Transport.

If the towpath is followed on the same bank, instead of crossing over via the bridge, it ends at the blocked Poplar Arm which was closed as late as 1982. Six-storey industrial buildings rise out of the canal, stretching for many yards along the waters edge.

The main canal takes a sharp corner to head west, the towpath being on the opposite bank via the turnover bridge. In an instant the perspective changes: old factories and workshops festooned with intricate pipework still line both banks, but there are clear hints of open areas to come. The buildings have turned their back on the canal but many on the non-towpath side still display the signs of an earlier time when boats were their transport system: doors on each floor to allow goods to be droped down to the boats below, mooring rings just above the water line.

A little further along, the enclosed atmosphere changes: now there is a great mixture of building types and sizes, between them views of distant

Canal Museum

churches and the Lace Market area. Nottingham city centre is reached after passing under the busy Carrington Street bridge with its decorative rosette panels, a good access point to the nearby rail station. Now there is an open area with grassy banks and seats, the towpath busy with local people using it as a pleasant short cut. On the far bank is the

Canal Museum, housed in an old warehouse of one of the most famous canal-carrying companies—Fellows, Morton and Clayton, the name given to the adjacent pub.[1]

The museum wharf was the scene of a terrible disaster in 1818, sudden death and destruction the appalling outcome. A ton of gunpowder was on the dock, stacked high in twenty-one barrels waiting for boat transport to the Derbyshire lead mines. A small amount of gunpowder leaked onto the ground and one of the boatmen thought it would make an entertaining flash if he dropped a hot clinker onto it. Entertaining it was not. The explosion killed eight men and two boys, and the mutilated body of the guilty boatman was thrown 100 yards across the canal. The warehouse was completely destroyed and most of the houses in the area were badly damaged. Two of the men killed were canal company employees: Job Barnes, a stonemason, and George Hayes, a labourer. Barnes' widow was paid 10s 6d a week until the company could decide who was responsible for meeting the cost of the disaster. Its insurance policy didn't cover such an unforeseen disaster and eventually legal action was taken against the employers of the blameworthy boatman, the Nottingham Boat Company.

Almost opposite the museum the towpath goes up and over a filled-in, and almost buried, bridge. An arm of the canal used to go under here and boats could float right into a large grain warehouse operated by the Midland Railway. Railway tracks entered at the other end of the building and grain cargoes could be transhipped without being spoilt by wet or windy weather. The warehouse was demolished and the canal arm filled in by 1982, now it is the site of a new Magistrates Court.

On the non-towpath side the bleak British Waterways' warehouse rises sheer from the canal. The grimy windows are broken, the paint is peeling, but when it was in use it must have been an imposing sight. The loading doors on each of the six floors form a reminder of the activity that took place here. Viewed from opposite the museum, it can be seen that the warehouse is wedge-shaped. This is because it was built between the canal and the now-filled-in Fothergill's Basin, the line of which can still be seen.[2]

The busy Wilford Street crosses the canal at the next bridge, with The Navigation pub at one end. This is not the original building, but in the canal's early years people came to the Navigation Tavern on this site to catch the regular packet-boat service to neighbouring towns and cities. For example, in 1798 a boat to Leicester used to leave here at 8am

1. *The entrance to the museum, and the trip-boat that operates from there, is in Canal Street via Carrington Street.*
2. *The warehouse may be restored for future office or leisure use.*

each weekday. Passengers and goods were booked in at the tavern and a cart went round the town gathering heavy items. The fares were:

First Room 5s, Second 2s.6d, Outside Passengers 1s.6d, goods 1s per cwt. Parcels at reasonable terms.

On Sundays there were pleasure trips, a reminder that the leisure use of canals is nothing new. Those who wanted to leave the town for some fresh air arrived at 2pm for a two-hour return cruise to the meadows at Beeston, at the western end of the canal.

Just above Castle Lock the stream Tinkers Leen flows next to the towpath, disappearing under the buildings to make its subterranean

Near Meadow Lane lock

way to the Trent. A bridge takes the towpath over an overflow weir, a method of controlling the canal's level, and excess water escapes into Tinkers Leen. Overflow systems are often forgotten, but are essential features of all man-made waterways. To save costs the canal engineers often used natural watercourses such as Tinkers Leen to take away excess supplies.

On the opposite bank is one of the modern buildings of which Nottingham is justifiably proud. Newcastle House, with its clean lines of blue glass and white stone, is an eye-catching change from the other commercial premises previously seen by this canal, and extraordinary if you know that the 'modern' Newcastle House was built in 1933. By the towpath a massive new building for the Inland Revenue is due for completion in 1995. Comparing the buildings on each bank, I must say I prefer the work of the 1930s architects.

The route through the city is very pleasant here. At weekends the towpath is amiably busy: local people fishing, jogging, cycling and strolling. A good compromise has been achieved between the two extremes of letting the old waterway decay or modernising it until a precious urban atmosphere is lost. Next to the towpath Tinkers Leen flows through banks lined with wild flowers. At first sight the habitat may look overgrown, but it is planned and managed to create shelter for city wildlife. The traffic beyond the buildings on the far side can be heard, but it's not intrusive, and those buildings do not always turn their backs to the canal. A good example is Castle Quay, new commercial buildings where coloured bricks have been used to achieve an agreeable effect: red, yellow, white and blue. With a tidily-mown grassy bank, and young trees planted, Castle Quay is a good example of what can be achieved along our old waterways.

In a series of shallow curves, lined with willows and poplars, the Nottingham & Beeston Canal does another of its congenial scene changes, from enclosed commercial to open retail and maritime. In the summer visiting boats are often moored here; the adjacent Sainsbury's is a handy opportunity for restocking with food and general supplies. Judging by the morning smells of frying bacon that waft up from the galleys, some of the food doesn't get very far. Nearby a large marina has permanent moorings for local craft and the entrance, under a towpath footbridge, is a tight bendy turn for the longer narrowboats.

From now on the canal retains interest by the effective method of changing the nature of its surroundings after every bridge, and the bridges are not far apart! The towpath side is often shielded by a grassy bank, but on the other side of the canal the variety is infinite. Before the road bridge by the marina are light commercial premises; after the bridge, a mixture of old and new housing, the end wall of one terrace resplendent with a large fish mural. Pass under the rail bridge and you find light industry both sides, but it is tree-lined and traffic noise is faint. The loudest noise I heard here on my last visit, a Saturday morning, was a tiny wren singing for all he was worth.

The next bridge carries Lenton Lane over the canal and is another towpath access point. This time the scene changes to moored boats on the opposite bank, an indication of the approach to Trevethick Boat Builders. Forget the glossy image of TV boatyards on the Solent, this is what they tend to look like on inland waterways: grey sheds surrounded by a jumble of nautical oddments, heaps of flotsam, and piles of jetsam;

everything you need to build any sort of craft, if only you could find what you were looking for. But all boatyards tend to have the same air about them, it's part of their charm. Trevethicks have been in business on this site since 1895, so whatever their system is, it obviously works well. Along the edge of the yard is a line of moored boats, some patiently await attention, others jaunty with new varnish and brasswork. At the western end of the yard is the entrance to the dry-dock, usually with one or two boats inside for repairs.

Not far beyond Trevethick's boatyard is an old waterway junction. Originally the Nottingham & Beeston Canal was two separate waterways: the Nottingham Canal owned by the Nottingham Canal Company, and the Beeston Cut owned by the Trent Navigation Company. By 1936 it was obvious that most of the Nottingham Canal was no longer required, so the Trent Navigation Company took over the remaining section and merged it with their Beeston Cut to form the Nottingham & Beeston Canal. Today, on the far side of the canal, a high bank of black piling rises out of the water, hiding the route the fifteen-mile-long Nottingham Canal once took into the coal-rich Erewash Valley. Now the River Leen has been diverted into the disused canal bed and, by climbing the grassy bank by the towpath, it can be seen flowing under the canal on its way to the Trent.

From now on the towpath follows what was the Beeston Cut of the Trent Navigation Company and evidence of the separate ownership can immediately be found. A few yards from the old junction there is a

NOTTINGHAM WATERWAYS PRIOR TO 1936

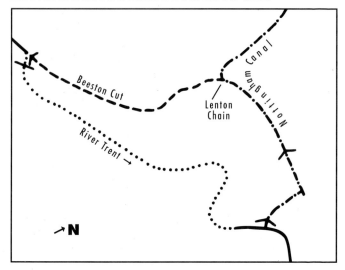

narrow, stone-lined section in the canal. This was the site of Lenton Chain. A canal company earned income from tolls levied on the boats using its waterway. This was easily defined—except where two canals in different ownership met at an unrestricted junction, as at Lenton. So, to stop boats from the other canal using their Beeston Cut without paying, the Trent Navigation Company narrowed their canal here so that a chain could be put across. In 1936 the two canals passed into the same ownership so the chain was no longer required. A few rusty links can still be seen on the stone-edging of the narrows.

The narrows at Lenton Chain is also a good place to prove that water does flow along a canal, it is not static as many people think. The rush of the water as it is forced through the narrows proves the point (as did the overflow weir above Castle Lock).

Another bridge, this time the A52 Ring Road, and another change of surroundings, but this time the bridge itself is interesting for the full-length mural of canal scenes painted on both banks. Homely back gardens give way to light industry, a smell of hot metal, stacked pallets and a typical canal view of various works. Trying to deduce what they produce, bend, mend, crush or brush gives a towpath walk an interesting extra dimension—but not for long on this ever-changing canal.

It's only a few yards from a modern bypass, soaring overhead, to a small brick bridge that looks lost. There is a little noise from the works on the far bank, but I've seen a heron here, watching a fisherman on the opposite bank. It was probably trying to work out why all that paraphernalia was needed to do something as simple as catching a fish. The peace soon returns and the canal is once again tree-lined as it curves below the brown towering chimneys of the Player's Horizon Factory, yet another of Nottingham's award-winning buildings.

Sloping landscaped lawns on the far bank are the grounds of one of Nottingham's most famous commercial names: Boots the chemist. A low, glass-walled office block can be seen before another bridge over the canal once again changes the atmosphere, this time literally—Boots chemical and pharmaceutical plant presents another industrial study, with silver patterns of intricate pipework, vents, ladders and vats; complicated but neat and tidy. A gentle hum emanates from the works: a combination of noise and smell.

Although it isn't noticeable, the canal has now turned to the south and is nearer to the River Trent, its ultimate destination. The Player's factory is the last feature on the near side and a wall now edges the towpath, protecting the canal from the Trent if the river floods across the sacrificial fields beyond. For the first time on this canal, the towpath here is unsurfaced and can be a little muddy after wet weather. However, it's still wide and easy to walk.

After the Boots works, the far bank changes to an open area and then to private gardens on the outskirts of the suburb of Beeston. This stretch is very pleasant, the air fresh from the Trent. It is possible to walk to the end of the canal on the same bank, but the towpath actually changes sides at a turnover bridge, now Canal Side Road. Bungalows and gardens, grassy banks, willows and seats line the last few yards to Beeston Lock and the River Trent.

Beeston

Beeston Lock is one of the locations where the striking difference between two types of waterway can most clearly be seen. The narrow, quiet, safe, Nottingham & Beeston Canal with its moored boats, lock, lock-house and gardens creates an ordered air of controlled water being used at will. Above the lock is the River Trent: wide, powerful, only condescending to supply a little of its waters to the canal, the majority roaring over the weir behind the lock-house. Follow the towpath from the canal and along the river bank and the whole atmosphere and temperature changes: fresher, cooler, cleaner, it is almost compulsory to take deep, lung-filling gulps of air.

The Trent sweeps round a tree-lined bend; on the far bank are open fields with hills rising beyond. In the far distance the towers of the obligatory power station, this one near the junction of the Trent, the River Soar and the Erewash Canal. All sorts of craft may be out here on the river—narrowboats, cruisers, yachts, canoes—all protected from the weir by a floating barrier across the Trent.

A footbridge across Beeston Lock gives access to a second lock, hidden and disused and at right-angles to the main one. This lock allowed boats to enter the Trent below the weir, but flood control measures have made the river unnavigable on that stretch and the old lock has not been used for many years. The stone-lined chamber is still there, and the grooves where the gates used to swing, but now the far end has flowers and a garden shed. The path down the side gives access to a vast, open, grassy area by the Trent, just below the weir. The amount of water coming over, the noise and the spray, depends on the weather of the previous days; if there has been heavy rain in the Midlands, the amount of fresh water coming down will be prodigious.

The unnavigable nature of the weir is the reason for the continued survival of the Nottingham & Beeston Canal, a waterway that surely packs more interest and variety into its six miles than any other.

A VIVID CONTRAST is provided by the now unnavigable section of the Nottingham Canal. Its coal-carrying role is now defunct and boats can no longer pass along the twelve miles from Lenton Chain to the Great Northern Basin at Langley Mill. The locks were at its southern end, in what are now Nottingham suburbs. From Wollaton it found the eastern flank of the Erewash valley, and kept its level by winding round to follow the contour in a style that even in the 1790s was old-fashioned engineering.

However, various lengths have survived and are still water-filled, the towpath often included in circular walks along the Erewash valley. A good example is north of Trowell where Broxtowe Borough Council has owned a section of the canal since 1977. A minor road links the A6096 and the A609, and just south of the mellow village of Cossall there is a lay-by with an information panel and a footbridge to the adjacent towpath. A little further south along the same road there is a car park at the clearly-signed 'Nottingham Canal Local Nature Reserve'. Another information panel and free leaflets describe the paths available, including two way-marked circular walks of three and five miles. For those a little less energetic the towpath provides a gentle stroll alongside the canal, here water-filled and bird-populated.

Most unnavigable canals are at their best in the spring, before summer reeds and bushes obscure the water channel. It's lovely here at that time—coots, moorhens and ducks dabble, and hedgerow birds sing. Walking north towards Cossall the junction with the Robinette's Arm can clearly be seen, a side-cut built to local collieries—in this area, everything to do with canals is everything to do with coal. From the towpath there are views across the mineral-rich Erewash valley, and sometimes glimpses of the parallel canal of the same name—like the Nottingham built to carry local coal to ever-wider markets. But times change. Coal is still carried along the valley, mainly to the Trent-side power stations, but the reason for the quietness of the towpath is signalled by the distant

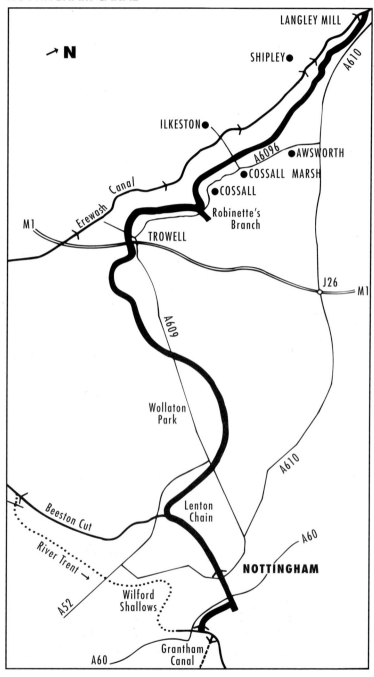

rumblings of the railway. Along the valley bottom, model-like 'merry-go-round' trains each carry over 1,000 tons of coal and are loaded and unloaded automatically without stopping—hence their name. It would have taken more than sixty boats to carry an equivalent load, and 60mph was out of the question!

With its only justification gone, the majority of the Nottingham Canal fell into disuse, the remaining lengths now peaceful reminders of an industrial past. At Langley Mill the last few yards form part of the Great Northern Basin, the boat-filled terminus of the Cromford Canal and the still-navigable Erewash Canal. At its southern end it has been usurped and retitled the Nottingham & Beeston Canal. At both ends the old canal still carries boats, as it was built to do, but the middle miles are the domain of the towpath walker.

Further Reading

Hadfield, Charles, *The Canals of the East Midlands* (David & Charles). History.

Useful Contacts

British Waterways Manager responsible for the canal. Tel: 0115 946 1017.
    Office by the side of Trent Lock, Erewash Canal.
Inland Waterways Association Tel: 0115 987 5475.

Boat Trips/Hire-Boats

Canal trips from the Canal Museum Tel: 0115 959 8835.

Angling (Main clubs, page 207)

Nottingham & Beeston Canal Popular fishery, particularly for large contests.
    Chub, roach, perch, bream, bleak.

Public Transport

Rail Stations (Nearest*) Nottingham*, Beeston, Langley Mill.

Places to Visit in the Area

Tourist Information Nottingham. Tel: 0115 947 0661.
Nottingham Canal Museum, Canal Street. Tel: 0115 959 8835.
Canal Local Nature Reserve, Cossall. Broxtowe Borough Council,
    Tel: 0115 925 4891.

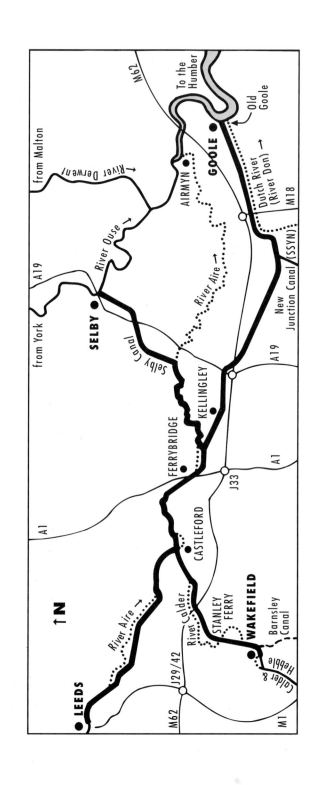

The Aire & Calder Navigation and The Selby Canal

Navigable

Main line: Leeds to Goole, 34 miles, 12 locks

Wakefield Branch: Wakefield to Castleford,
7 miles, 4 locks

Selby Canal (and river access to): 11 miles, 4 locks

OS maps: Landranger sheets 104, 105, 110, 111

THE *Aire & Calder is a bold navigation—confident, muscular and proud. Not for this waterway the quiet, diffident air exuded by many others as they tiptoe through the countryside, the backwaters of another age. No—the Aire & Calder strides across Yorkshire, a burly bastion of modern commercial carrying.*

As a waterway used for many centuries, the A&C offers a wide variety of places to visit. In Leeds there are weekend markets, boat trips, towpath walks, brewery tours, and soon the Royal Armouries. A riverside pub at Ferrybridge is a good place to watch the working boats, and sea-going ships can be seen in the port of Goole via a public footpath that crosses the immense Ocean Lock. On a quieter note, the little-used Selby Canal has a towpath through open countryside, a basin with a swing-bridge, and a lock into the tidal River Ouse.

The Aire & Calder is a typical river navigation. Over the centuries various artificial channels have been cut, and now river and canal intertwine, locks bypassing weirs and shallows. The termini of the two western arms are at Leeds on the River Aire, and Wakefield on the River Calder—hence the name. The Calder flows into the Aire at Castleford, and the merged navigation continues eastward until just past Ferrybridge. At Bank Dole Junction it splits to give access to two ports on the River Ouse: boats going to the docks at Goole leave the river and turn onto a broad canal; those going to Selby use the River Aire a little further to find the Selby Canal. The last few miles of the river are no longer used for navigation because of their bendy, muddy nature.

IN LEEDS the River Aire rushes through the gloomy man-made caverns of 'the dark arches', only half-seen by the visitors, many of whom give its subterranean waters a wary glance. Unlikely as it may seem, this is the entrance to Granary Wharf, a popular waterside area with boat-trips, locks, fishing, a picnic area, specialist shops open every day, a craft market on Fridays and weekends, street entertainers, and a car park in the midst of which boats are often being repaired in dry-docks![1]

The canal basin beyond the arches is the meeting point of two water-ways that link to cross the country from coast to coast. The spectacular Leeds & Liverpool Canal goes westward to cross the Pennines to

LEEDS

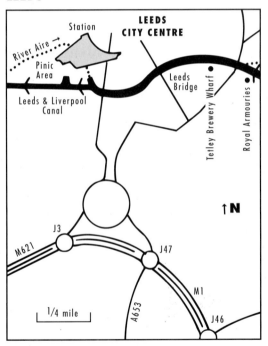

1. *Follow 'City Centre' signs from the M1, Junction 47. The entrance is under the large railway viaduct where it passes over Neville Street. Ample parking is available here, or follow the 'Granary Wharf' signs on approach. Leeds rail station is two minutes' walk away.*

Merseyside, the River Aire goes eastward to become the Aire & Calder Navigation to Humberside. The popular grassy waterside area of Granary Wharf is between two locks—Office Lock starts the Leeds & Liverpool's climb towards Lancashire; River Lock takes boats down to the River Aire after its emergence from the dark arches. The trip-boat descends River Lock before cruising along the waterfront area that in the 1800s was so busy with working boats, taking on and landing cargoes, that it was almost possible to walk across the river.

The old riverside warehouses were the centre of Leeds' transport system, vital components in the city's thriving trade. After the railways came, Leeds gradually turned its back on the river, but over the last few years the waterway's leisure potential has been recognised. Many of the old warehouses are still by the river and still play their part in the commerce of Leeds, but now they have been converted into much-sought-after offices. From the trip-boat it is obvious that much has been done to improve the waterfront areas: a walkway is spreading along the river banks, more sections are being incorporated into new building designs, and popular attractions such as Tetley's Brewery Wharf have been added. The trip-boat calls here, as it will at the Royal Armouries when that museum opens in 1996.

If, instead of going back, the trip-boat carried on along the Navigation for another sixteen miles it would reach Ferrybridge. Here the customers at the Golden Lion have a grand view of the cargo-carrying boats, the tugs pushing and pulling like patient shire horses, delivering their loads without fuss or celebration. Throughout every weekday the tugs leave Kellingley Colliery pushing 500 tons of coal before them, the load carried in three separate linked containers called 'pans'. The whole operation seems effortless, and it is easy to overlook the skill of the boatmen as they control tug and pans with a total length of 195 feet. The coal is bound for the ever-hungry Ferrybridge power station, its looming cooling towers dwarfing everything in sight. When they arrive there, the pans are separated before each is lifted out of the water and its load removed by turning the vessel upside down. This hoist, called the 'tippler', is one of only two of its kind in the world. When three pans have been emptied they are linked together again and the tug—pulling this time—takes its unruly charges back to the colliery for reloading.

The Golden Lion is by Ferrybridge flood-lock, through which all vessels have to pass.[2] In addition to the coal 'trains' you may also see 650-ton tankers, barges carrying gravel, and dwarfed pleasure craft. The footbridge over the lock gives access to a path on the bank between the

2. *North-east of Pontefract, on the B6136 at Ferrybridge where it passes under the A1 flyover.*

Granary Wharf

two water courses: the River Aire and the canal section. The walk is away from the A1 bridge with its traffic noise, although this becomes less obtrusive after a while because there is much of interest to see here.

Tanker at Ferrybridge

In the shadow of the A1's modern flyover is the lovely old bridge which used to carry traffic on the Great North Road in the nineteenth century. It can only be crossed on foot now, but the names of its architect and builders are still proudly marked in the wall at the centre of the span. For all its charm, the old bridge is a navigational hazard for the large commercial vessels, especially when the river is flowing strongly in the winter or spring. It is however a listed structure, so the working boatmen coming downstream have to use their skill to thread their monster craft through its arches, and then make a tight turn before lining up an accurate approach to the flood-lock's narrow chamber. There's no lack of entertainment for customers at the pub's riverside tables.

In past centuries many of the cargoes were carried to Selby, the A&C Navigation Company's first man-made port. Originally the main reason for the development of the waterway was to give the trade of Leeds and Wakefield access to east-coast shipping. In the 1770s, sea-going ships could reach sixty miles inland to Selby on the River Ouse, so the Navigation Company built a five-mile canal to take their boats from the River Aire to the inland port. Now the Selby Canal is a quiet little waterway used only by pleasure craft, but in its time it was busy with working boats and Selby thrived on the trade it carried. It's a difficult scene to envisage now, as the town has developed away from the canal, leaving the small basin and its swing-bridge to today's leisure boaters. It is however still an inland port, as shown by the lockside anti-rabies sign in various languages.

Beyond the lock the River Ouse swirls and flows—from left to right usually, but right to left when the tide rushes in. All tidal waters that come via the Humber Estuary are full of mud and silt, and when this is deposited it causes many problems. The Ouse leaves tons of it in mud-banks at the entrance to Selby Lock and these can be seen at low water, another difficulty for boats crossing the swift currents to enter the chamber. Sometimes the lock-keeper has to climb down to fend a boat off from the stone walls. When all is safely gathered in, the lock gates are closed by a combination of windlass and chains—the keeper pushes the windlass round and the chains pull the gates open or shut. The agile part of his job is stepping over the chain on every circuit without losing momentum! But this old system is slow and if British Waterways can find the funding, Selby lock will be changed to powered operation: mundane, but a faster method of gathering boats into the safety of the canal from the powerful river. Boats can only use Selby Lock when the tide is right, so activity is spasmodic; more often than not visitors have to imagine how the windlass and chain system works.

The towpath of the Selby Canal is now a quiet passage through rich rural countryside, its five miles a popular route, especially the part that is included in the circular nine-mile Selby Horseshoe walk.[3] The reason for the solitude on the canal is that trade continued to thrive on the Aire & Calder Navigation and it soon became obvious that the single basin and lock at Selby, as the only outlet to the Ouse and the sea, were inadequate. So the Navigation Company decided to replace Selby, its canal and its lock, by building yet another port, and another canal to link the River Aire to it—Goole was the result.

The small village of Old Goole had been there for centuries but in the 1820s the confident Aire & Calder Navigation Company decided to build a complex of basins and locks nearby, where its new canal met the River Ouse—and not only that, it went on to create the nucleus of present-day Goole as a new town to house its staff.

Today the port is thriving. Barges and tankers still bring their cargoes

3. *A Selby Horseshoe walk leaflet is available from the town's Tourist Information.*

Selby Canal

along the canal, but the majority of the goods handled at Goole are carried in sea-going ships. The docks are a fascinating place to visit—a one-hour circular walk will reveal ships, Ocean Lock, dry-docks, swing-bridges, warehouses, and a mural of the port in its early sailing ship days. Don't forget the binoculars.[4]

Aire Street is the oldest part of the town, the buildings created with the original docks. Upstairs in the Lowther Hotel a large recently-renovated mural shows the scene as it was then—cargoes being moved by crane between graceful sailing ships and canal boats and warehouses. It's the only surviving picture of the port's early days, apart from some etchings, and the hotel's owner is happy to show the mural to visitors.

By the Lowther Hotel is the start of a public footpath that goes through the docks, the boundaries of which are marked by two yellow lines painted on the ground. On weekdays beeping fork-lifts scurry about, moving loads between the warehouses that line the path. Lorries come

---

4. *Follow 'Town Centre' signs from Junction 36 of the M62. At the roundabout with a clock tower in the centre, follow signs 'The Docks' into North Street and Aire Street.*

THE PORT OF GOOLE

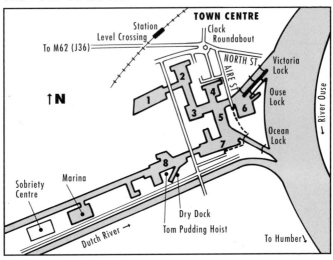

1. West Dock
2. Stanhope Dock
3. Railway Dock
4. Aldam Dock

5. Ship Dock
6. Ouse Dock
7. Barge Dock
8. South Dock

and go and all is activity. Summer evenings are a good time to visit the docks because it is quiet but there are still many ships to see, fast turnround times mean the docks are often emptier at weekends. Between rows of warehouses stacked with timber, the path eventually reaches Ocean Lock and if the tide is right there's every chance of a grandstand view of a ship passing through. At other times the walk is still a rare opportunity to see an island nation's import–export trade in action— and the varied national ensigns and ports of registration of the ships.

Vià the path and public roads, all parts of the docks can be seen at close quarters. With all the maritime influences it is easy to forget that the port is an inland waterway—the creation of the Aire & Calder Navigation Company. A reminder of that fact is the one remaining Tom Pudding hoist that towers over South Dock, a forerunner of the tippler now used at Ferrybridge power station. To a large extent, the profits of the Navigation Company were based on coal, which was carried it along the river and canal to Goole where it was loaded into ships for export. In the 1860s the A&C developed a system of tugs to pull trains of compartment boats, each part of which was lifted up by a hoist—such as the one by South Dock—and tilted so that the coal was emptied into a ship moored beneath. This system was so successful it lasted until 1986.

Sea-going ship in Goole docks

A short film was made of the Tom Pudding system in action at Goole and this can be seen at the Sobriety Waterways Adventure Centre and Museum.

The Sobriety Centre is on the bank between the Aire & Calder Navigation and an earlier artificial waterway, the Dutch River. Dug in the 1630s, the Dutch River is the man-made outlet of the River Don, its waters flowing down from Sheffield, Rotherham and Doncaster. It looks insignificant now—ignored by the craft on the canal and in the docks—but it was the original way for boats to sail to inland towns and as such is the reason why all the other waterway developments took place here. Without the Dutch River, Goole would not exist.

Further Reading

Calder Navigation Society, *West Yorkshire Waterway Guide*
(1992; ISBN 0-9512400-1-3; available from the Society, see below).
Hadfield, Charles, *The Canals of Yorkshire and North East England*
(David & Charles). History.
Smith, Peter L., *The Aire & Calder Navigation* (Wakefield Historical
Publications, 1987; ISBN 0-901869-27-9). History.

Useful Contacts

Calder Navigation Society 3 Elm Way, Birstall, Batley WF17 0EQ.
Tel: 01924 477571.
British Waterways Manager responsible for the Aire & Calder Navigation.
Tel: 01977 516329. The manager of the Selby Canal. Tel: 01904 728229.

Boat Trips/Hire-Boats

Yorkshire Hire Cruisers Leeds. Party bookings on *Kirkstall Flyboat*.
Tel: 0113 2456195.
Banks Hire-Boats Selby. Narrowboats for hire. Tel: 01347 821772.
Sobriety Centre Goole. Pre-booked tours of Goole Docks or along the canal,
for small parties. See page 67.

Angling (Main clubs, page 205)

Aire & Calder A developing fishery recovering from a long history of pollution.
Roach, perch, gudgeon, bream.
Granary Wharf Leeds. Permits from the car park entrance kiosk.
Selby Canal Popular fishery, particularly for angling contests. Roach, perch,
bream, chub.

Public Transport

Rail Stations (Nearest*) Leeds*, Wakefield-Westgate, Castleford, Selby, Goole.

Places to Visit in the Area

Tourist Information Leeds, Tel: 0113 247 8301.Goole, Tel: 01405 762187.
Leeds A large number of attractions, including:
   Granary Wharf 30 craft shops and markets

Tetley's Brewery Wharf Brewery tour, other displays, shire horses, museum, pub of the future. Pre-booking not essential but advisable. Tel: 0113 242 0666.

Armley Mills Once the world's largest woollen mill, steam engines, picnic area, giant mill wheel, 1920s cinema. Tel: 0113 263 7861.

Thwaite Mills Museum Tel: 0113 249 1453.

Sobriety Waterways Adventure Centre and Museum Dutch Riverside, Goole DN14 5TB. Open Mon–Fri, 08.30–16.00, most weeks of the year. Admission free. 1.5 miles from town centre. Tel: 01405 768730.

Drax Power Station Near Selby. Western Europe's largest coal-fired station. Guided coach and walking tour, by prior arrangement only, minimum age for children 10. Tel: 01757 618381.

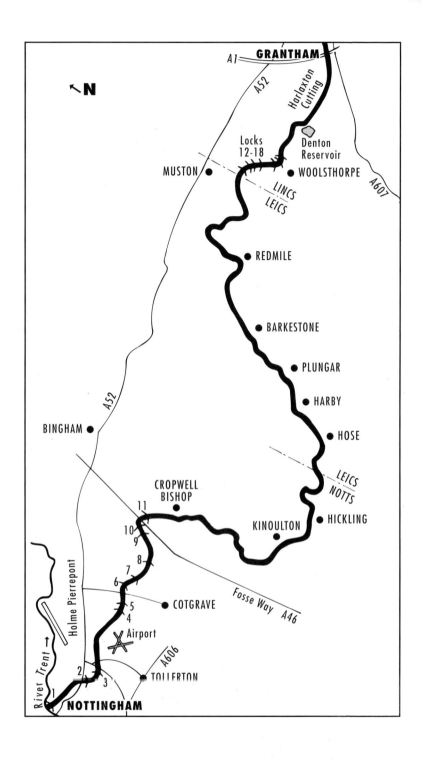

The Grantham Canal

Unnavigable, but restoration started
33 miles long, 18 wide locks
OS maps: Landranger sheets 129, 130

THE Grantham Canal is a rare thing: an English waterway of more than moderate length that keeps one character throughout—and that character is quiet rural charm. Yes, it's true that one end of the canal is in the city of Nottingham, the other in Grantham, but between those two urban areas it passes through almost thirty miles of gently rolling country-side in three counties—Nottinghamshire, Leicestershire and Lincolnshire. It borders rich arable fields and unspoilt villages and eventually reaches the heart of the Vale of Belvoir. A peaceful distance away from main roads, it is a waterway for strolling and allowing the cares of the week to float away into the open acres.

Access to the canal is from country lanes, many access points are equipped with car parks, picnic areas and information boards, and restoration work is making the waterway navigable again. The old locks have been sur-rounded with post-and-rail fences to make them safer, although the design does not prevent small children from reaching the chamber edges. The principal attraction for visitors is the Grantham Canal's magnificent towpath, one of the best in the country; it is wide, level, well drained and usually covered by neatly-mown grass. Alongside is a canal full of water, the result of British Waterways' maintaining it as an important part of the land drainage system, even though it was abandoned for boat use in 1936. The only dry section is four miles long near Cropwell Bishop, the porous gypsum beds beneath the channel causing water-retention problems *since the canal was built in the 1790s. The overall result is easy walking along a quiet waterway, with abundant wildlife, through mind-unwinding countryside.*

FROM the River Trent at Nottingham the canal climbs 140 feet to the summit pound at Grantham, climbing via eighteen locks clustered at both ends of the waterway. Inbetween the two groups of locks, the canal is level for twenty miles, gently curving to keep to the 150ft contour.

The entrance lock near Nottingham Forest football ground

The junction with the Trent has survived; the entrance lock to the Grantham Canal is just downstream from Trent Bridge at the side of the Nottingham Forest football ground. To find the lock is a pleasant walk along the river and past the clubhouses of various canoeing and rowing organisations, although it's not so quiet when Forest are playing at home. The lock from the river has survived, but it is not usable and extra gates have been installed and sealed as a precaution against high levels in the Trent flooding back along the canal.

JUNCTION WITH THE RIVER TRENT AT NOTTINGHAM

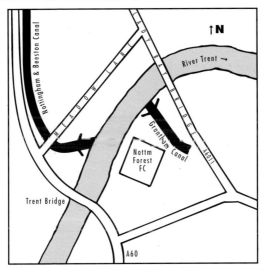

New roads and other obstructions mean that restoration of the canal through here is very unlikely; instead plans are being made for a new route.

On the opposite bank of the Trent is the entrance to the Meadow Lane lock of the Nottingham & Beeston Canal, almost all river craft entering to bypass a weir further up river. For many years working boats crossed the Trent between the two canals—agricultural produce from the Grantham Canal to the rapidly-growing city of Nottingham; in the opposite direction coal from the Erewash valley and the obnoxious 'nightsoil' from Nottingham's earth closets. This malodorous cargo was carried in 'sani-boats' and dug into the farming land alongside the Grantham Canal as fertiliser; many fragments of white clay smoking pipes are still found in these fields, the remains of the 'deposits'. There was probably less leisure walking of the towpath at that time!

From the entrance lock the towpath can be walked for a few yards, but the link with the rest of the waterway has been severed by new roads. As a result, the most convenient place to find the Grantham Canal near Nottingham is where it is crossed by the Tollerton Road at Bridge 7, north-west of the fields that form the grandly-named Nottingham Airport.

The rural nature of the waterway starts here and lasts all the way to Grantham; a drive along the canal and through the unspoilt villages with some quiet towpath walks is a pleasant way to spend a day. There is a good booklet of circular walks for the Nottinghamshire end of the canal; car parks, picnic sites and very good information panels have been provided and the walks have been marked by a special logo.[1]

Towpath logo

Access is possible and pleasant from nearly all the quiet country lanes that cross the canal and it would be repetitive to list them all. Therefore, I have included only those of some special note, but that does not mean other locations should be ignored; rather the opposite, the secluded Grantham Canal is a waterway to explore and discover for oneself with, perhaps, the following as initial pointers.

A good example is Bridge 12—north of Cotgrave on the road to the A52—where there's a car park, an information panel and a wheelchair-wide path to two locks; at No. 4, the farthest from the road, there are picnic tables and a lock-keeper's cottage. This lock, also known as 'Skinner's', is typical of many on the canal and the water runs unimpeded through a gateless chamber, brick-lined and edged with mellow stone. Below the lock the cottage garden borders the towpath and a feature has been made of a feeder stream flowing through to the canal.

The only main road that crosses the canal's central section is the Fosse Way (A46) at Bridge 18. It is a pity the site is not signed on the road because it is a pleasant spot with one of the few original brick bridges remaining on this canal and Lock 11 (Fosse Top) is the last of the flight that has climbed up from the River Trent. Eastwards from here the canal is level for twenty miles. At such a location, where a navigable waterway was crossed by a road of some importance, there was invariably a wharf so that goods could be transhipped between the two transport systems,

1. *Discover the Grantham Canal. See page 75 for details.*

as well as taken to nearby villages. Here the wharf covered the well-tended grassy area by the lock and at the end of the stone-edging is a set of well-used steps down to water level. Not that a boat could call here now, as this is part of the four-mile dry section; the canal bed in this area is so porous it has defied two centuries of efforts to keep it watertight. The channel is obvious but it's as dry as bone, no sign of the damp-loving plants that usually find a little water in the bottom of unused canals. I've taken a great liking to Lock 11, although I'm not sure why—an honourable old lock, grass-carpeted and sheltering wild flowers, but not overgrown: a rare mixture.

By the time the canal reaches Kinoulton it's again holding water, still reedy and shallow, but conditions improve at Hickling where it widens out into a roadside basin. Restoration work in 1994 has made a tremendous difference here, and beyond the basin three new swing-bridges carry farm roads over the dredged canal. The warehouse on the south side is one the canal's few original buildings and now boats can once again tie up alongside, although it must be admitted that the main

Hickling basin

function of the basin's visitors is feeding the voracious ducks—not forgetting the swans, cygnets, sparrows and any other feathered resident. Reveal a bag of bread and you could be mugged by a Hickling duckling! The information panel tells of village children traditionally hearing of a huge whale that comes up the canal at midnight to turn round in the basin. I don't think it's true—the ducks would eat it!

The Grantham Canal now crosses into Leicestershire, its winding course a classic sign of a man-made waterway following a contour to maintain a level rather than taking a direct line via flights of locks. This is perhaps the quietest section; even the lovely old villages of Hose,

Harby, Barkestone and Plungar are bypassed on the approach to the Vale of Belvoir and its proud castle.

On the road between Harby and Plungar is Bridge 45 at Stathern Wharf. This is the quietest roadside stop I've found on the canal; there's a small picnic site—no tables but it's nicely mown—an old humpback bridge, and of course the Grantham Canal's magnificent towpath. This really is the heart of England; the tranquil fields roll to the horizon, the birds sing, and a nice cup of tea is just up the road. 'Our Little Farm' is by the canal on the outskirts of Plungar; traditional farm animals in traditional farm buildings, and a tea-room in an old cowshed.

Belvoir Castle is less than two miles away, high on a hill to the south, as the canal enters Lincolnshire and starts its final rise to Grantham; Lock 12, by a bridge on the Muston–Stenwith road, marks the end of the twenty-mile pound. Two more locks, 16 and 17, are by the Rutland Arms, a popular pub with a children's play area, camping and sometimes canoe rallies.[2] More restoration work has made these locks usable again, another piece of the scheme that will one day make the whole canal navigable. The scenery is less open now as the canal approaches a ridge on the final approach to Grantham, soon to enter the wooded Harlaxton Cutting.

As always, an often-missed aspect is a canal's water supply; Denton Reservoir is reachable from Denton, a public footpath surrounds its 61 million gallons and the open area over the water is very different to the nearby canal in Harlaxton Cutting with trees forming a canopy overhead. Lovely old nineteenth-century brick bridges take quiet lanes over the waterway and the delightfully enclosed atmosphere is different to anywhere else on the Grantham Canal.[3] Walking in the cutting—or boating when the restoration schemes succeed—it is difficult to comprehend that it's only one mile to where the A1 brutally cuts across the canal and severs the link with its name town.

On the positive side, the A1 does make it easy to reach this end of the Grantham Canal and enjoy its simple pleasures. In Grantham the canal basin has been lost, but for those who enjoy a treasure hunt some isolated sections can be found; from the A1 the A607 approaches the town centre, by turning left from it at Trent Road, and further on the A607 at Earlesfield Lane, the canal can be found where the two roads bridge the old waterway.

It's a long way from the River Trent: 33 miles and two counties away via a charming waterway with a marvellous towpath—The Grantham Canal.

2. *North of the village Woolsthorpe by Belvoir, off the road to Stenwith and Muston.*
3. *One such bridge is No. 66, on the road between Harlaxton and Barrowby.*

Further Reading

Hadfield, Charles, *The Canals of the East Midlands* (David & Charles). History.
Robinson, David N., *Lincolnshire Boats and Bridges in Camera* (Quotes Ltd, 1989; ISBN 0-86023-365-0). Old photographs.
Discover the Grantham Canal (£3.75, 85 pages; available from The Rights of Way Section, Department of Planning and Economic Development, Nottinghamshire County Council, Trent Bridge House, Fox Road, West Bridgford, Nottingham NG2 6BJ, Tel: 0115 977 4483). Free leaflets about the canal may also be available.

Useful Contacts

British Waterways Manager responsible for the canal. Tel: 0115 946 1017. Office by the side of Trent Lock, Erewash Canal.
Grantham Canal Restoration Society 3 Barratt Crescent, Attenborough, Nottingham NG9 6HA. Tel: 0115 922 7311.
Grantham Navigation Association Alexandra House, 1 Willesden Green, Nuttall, Notts NG16 1QF. Tel: 0115 979 4491.

Angling

At the Nottingham end the fishing is excellent and day tickets are available. Tench, bream, roach, carp.

Public Transport

Rail Stations Nottingham, Grantham.

Places to Visit in the Area

Tourist Information Grantham. Tel: 01476 66444.
Holme Pierrepont Country Park and National Water Sports Centre Nottingham. Tel: 0115 982 1212.
Our Little Farm By the canal, south-west of Plungar. Farmyard animals, rare breeds, nature trail, tea-room, shop. Tel: 01949 60349.
Belvoir Castle Near Grantham. Home of the Duke and Duchess of Rutland. Castle rooms, gardens, special events, jousting. Dogs not allowed in house or gardens. Tel: 01476 870262.

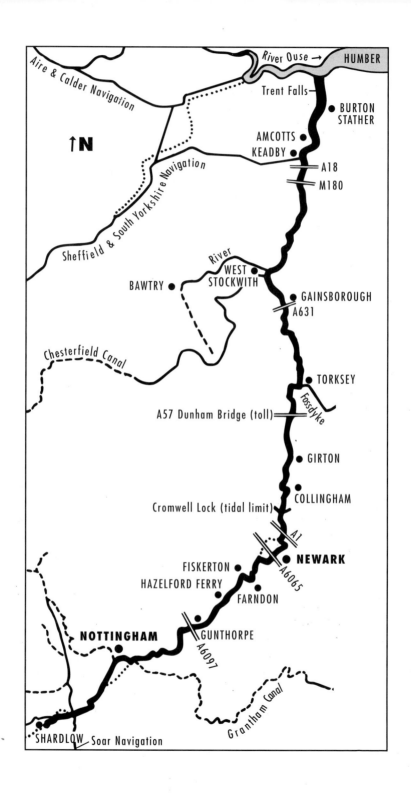

The River Trent

170 miles long, 93 miles covered by this book
Navigable between Shardlow and Trent Falls
12 wide locks
OS map: Landranger sheets 129, 120, 121, 112

THE Trent is England's third longest river, flowing 170 miles from north Staffordshire to the Humber estuary. Above Shardlow in Derbyshire the river is too small for navigation. Instead, boats must enter the adjacent Trent & Mersey Canal to reach the famous towns further upstream such as Burton-on-Trent and Stoke-on-Trent, and to gain access to the rest of the canal system.

This book covers the navigable section of the Trent—downstream from Shardlow where the river's 93 miles are the central thread of the waterways' system. Within those miles, the Trent is a river of great variety, almost straining belief that it is one waterway. From the popular marina and locks at Sawley, it flows under the famous Trent Bridge, through Nottingham's rowing-club-lined banks, alongside Newark's castle, down Cromwell Weir to become a tidal river, through prudent flood-meadows, past the shipping wharves at Gainsborough and Keadby, and finally to the Humber in mud-banked seclusion at Trent Falls.

Little that we see today is natural river; the Trent is too important for that. Throughout recorded history it has been a trading artery with man striving to improve its navigable qualities—to take his larger and larger boats further upstream. The modern Trent is based on the major engineering schemes carried out in the 1790s. Greater water depth is achieved by the level being held up by weirs spaced throughout the 38 miles from

Sawley to Cromwell, each weir having a lock for boats to navigate the change of level.

But no matter how beneficial the Trent's use for water transport may be, navigational improvements must never interfere with the river's most important function—the drainage of a vast area of England. Six million people rely on the Trent and its many tributaries for the natural drainage of the 6,500 square miles in which they live. Therefore, where the construction of a lock would narrow the river too much, an artificial channel is made called a 'cut'. The lock and other navigational paraphernalia is built in the channel—as in Sawley Cut and Cranfleet Cut—and the river is left free to bypass it by flowing along its true course.

Cromwell, as the furthest downstream weir and lock, is where the Trent undergoes its greatest transformation. Above the weir it is a man-controlled deep river, as it has been since leaving Sawley—lined by towns and villages. Below Cromwell Weir the Trent is open to the sea, its last fifty miles subject to natural tidal forces. As a result, the river immediately becomes more remote, most buildings keeping their distance behind flood defences—meadows, walls and banks.

WEST OF Nottingham the Trent has a cluster of busy boating sites popular with visitors—within ten road miles there's Shardlow's eighteenth-century inland port; Sawley marina and locks; Trent Lock at the end of the Erewash Canal; the lakes of the Attenborough Nature Reserve, and the Nottingham & Beeston Canal.

Shardlow is the Trent's head of navigation, 94 miles from the end of the river. There's a marina for local boats, but craft passing through enter the Trent & Mersey Canal a little further downstream. Shardlow's location, where the river and canal are crossed by a busy road (A6), made it into a prominent inland port—much of which survives today. Walking along the canal towpath it's easy to imagine the noise and activity that bustled here until the 1850s. The boatyards are now busy with pleasure craft but the surroundings are of a commercial age—old warehouses and stores, large houses built for the merchants, boat-horse stables, workers' cottages, pubs and shops, a lock and a lock-house. This fascinating example of another transport age is best explored on foot, and a useful leaflet is available from the Arkwright Society.

Less than one mile along the towpath, past one more lock, is the end of the canal and boats enter the river proper. This is quite a significant waterways' junction as it is also where the Trent meets the River Derwent flowing down from Derby.

RIVER TRENT WEST OF NOTTINGHAM

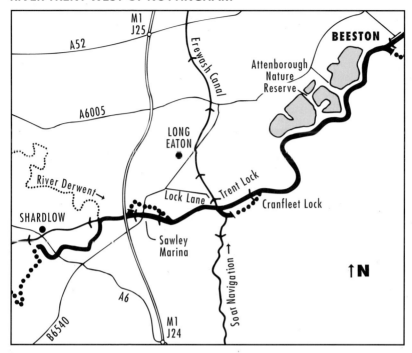

The next section of the Trent is familiar to millions of people; the weir and the entrance to the avoiding Sawley Cut are easily seen from the M1 as the motorway soars across the river.

The sheltered Sawley Cut is on the B6540, only a few minutes' drive from Shardlow. The large marina has a chandlery/gift shop, tea-rooms, restaurant and toilets. The towpath on the opposite bank is usually boat-lined and it's a pleasant short walk to the locks where the Cut drops to the level of the rejoining weir-lowered river. There are two locks, side by side—necessary as the number of boats wanting to pass through is very high on summer weekends.

Less than a mile further north on the B6540, on the south side of Long Eaton, is Lock Lane. This road goes down to the river at Trent Lock, where it is joined by the Erewash Canal. With its pubs, picnic tables and boat activity, this is always a very popular spot, especially on summer weekend afternoons.[1] The Trent is wide here because it is an important waterways' junction—boats can turn towards the north along the Erewash Canal, or to Leicester and the south by turning into

---

1. *Trent Lock is in the 'Erewash Canal' chapter.*

the River Soar. The Trent itself divides, most of the flow going over a weir, the remainder into the Cranfleet Cut with its lock at the far end. Because of its complexity, the junction is equipped with road-type signs—turn left for here, turn right for there, and no-entry. The Trent, having absorbed substantial volumes of water from the Derwent and the Soar, has now swollen to become the principal waterway of the East Midlands.

On the far bank the land rises up to form the hills that keep the Trent in its place between here and Nottingham. Red Hill does its best to hide Ratcliffe power station, one of the largest in the country. This area is also one end of an official long-distance walk, the Trent Valley Way—the other end is 84 miles away at West Stockwith. Nottinghamshire County Council has published a guide booklet and leaflets on circular walks and cycle routes along the River Trent.

Four miles away by road is the riverside Attenborough Nature Reserve. Thousands of birds visit the three miles of lakes, and the site is one of the UK's most important nesting areas. There is a network of footpaths around the lakes and along the river, good fishing, information panels, a large lakeside car park, but no toilets. Attenborough is a good example of industry and nature working together because the lakes are flooded gravel pits, and the work is still taking place. Topsoil is removed and stored, and the uncovered gravel is mechanically dug and loaded into small barges for transport to the grading and mixing site. About half of the lakes have been allocated to the nature reserve—others have been filled in, covered with the stored topsoil, and returned to agricultural use.

A little further downstream the Trent plummets over another weir, this one avoided by the Nottingham & Beeston Canal. The grassy fields below the weir are a refreshing place to be on a hot summer day and the nearby lock is the usual magnet for boats and their watchers. The canal takes vessels through the centre of Nottingham, returning them to the river a short distance below Trent Bridge.[2]

The river makes its own way through Nottingham—flowing at the foot of wooded hills at Clifton, and under an old toll-bridge at Wilford where the boards announcing the charges are still shown on the tollhouse.

The terraced and tree-lined Victoria Embankment provides a congenial approach to the famous Trent Bridge. Both banks are good strolling areas, the link between them a suspension footbridge that springs with each step. The boats normally seen here are from the rowing clubs that have their headquarters a little further downstream—individuals in skiffs and sculls skitter across the surface, lightweight contrasts to the muscle-bulging teamwork of the rowing-eights. But on four days each year

2. *A description of the lock and weir area is in the 'Nottingham & Beeston Canal' chapter.*

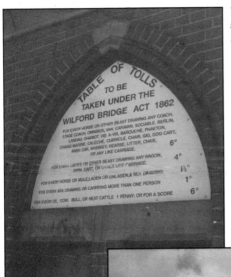

The toll-house on Wilford Bridge still displays the payments that were levied to cross the Trent

Suspension footbridge, Victoria Embankment

these embankments are lined with a diverse mass of vessels, a colourful backdrop to the Nottingham Boat Show, a national event attracting hundreds of exhibitors and thousands of public visitors.

The current Trent Bridge was built in 1871 and it is a structure which manages to look both elegant and sturdy, not an easily-achieved combination. The ornamental cast ironwork is painted in different colours and the bridge is worthy of its fame, known throughout the cricketing world because of the nearby Test Match ground. It is a memorable crossing of the river on a fine summer Saturday morning when England are playing Australia at Trent Bridge. Crowds of spectators swarm over. The pavements fill with groups excitedly chattering about the coming day's play, all making their way to the south bank. What marks this out as a cricket crowd are the trappings they lug about—large picnic hampers, cushions, binoculars, packets of sandwiches, flasks of drinks, radios with earpieces, stuffed kangaroos, and bulging shoulder-bags hiding goodness knows what. It's an exciting time to be by the River Trent.

Back into the quiet world of waterways, the riverside path continues along the south bank. The clubhouses of various rowing organisations line the river; at weekends or on summer evenings their members are usually clambering down to the water festooned in colourful vests, crafts and oars. Across the river the Nottingham & Beeston Canal rejoins, most powered vessels diverting into the lock to continue their passage upstream. It's a pity that Trent Bridge is on a navigational dead-end, but the reason is a legacy from its predecessor. The old bridge had very narrow arches and caused considerable problems for the engineless boats trying to pass beneath. This was a curtailment of trade, so one of the reasons for building the canal was to make a boating bypass of the old bridge, its constricted channels and the dangerous currents that surged through them.

The cricket crowds may fill the area in the summer, but on winter Saturday afternoons it's football fans that congregate by the river. The surprisingly elegant floodlight towers of Notts County FC can be seen just beyond the buildings on the north bank. Almost opposite is Nottingham Forest's ground, bounded on one side by the Trent, on another by the Grantham Canal. Until 1875 there used to be a bridge across the Trent here, a somewhat fragile structure on which horses pulled boats between the two canals on opposing banks—the Grantham and the Nottingham & Beeston.

Bridges and locks are obvious features, but a crucial aspect of the river that is seldom noticed is the flood controls that protect Nottingham. Since flowing over the weir at Beeston, the Trent has been flanked by often unobtrusive restrictions—banking and walls set back from the river's normal course so that excess water can spread to delegated sacrificial areas. In the past Trent floods have done great damage in Nottingham but now over 29,000 properties are protected. The major part of the scheme is the sluice-gates at Holme, two and a half miles downstream from Trent Bridge. Five gates, each forty feet wide, control the river and are normally set to increase water depth by eleven feet to aid navigation. But in times of flood the gates can be opened fully to allow excess water to escape downriver. Sluices may be mundane, but the effect on the river and the surrounding area is profound.

On the north bank the deepened river maintains the lakes of Colwick Country Park, and on the south bank provides the water for the National Watersports Centre at Holme Pierrepont. Open to the public and set in grassy parkland, the National Watersports Centre has a variety of attractions. There are nature trails in the park, an information centre, food, toilets, and plenty of parking spaces. Signposted from Nottingham, the Centre is easy to find just south of the Trent, and on arrival the signs for the slalom course lead to a pleasant car park on the edge of the river. The Centre was opened in 1972 to re-use worked out gravel pits, now transformed into lakes, where the public can try every form of 'on the water' activity, but not swimming. Dinghy sailing, rowing, power boating, water-skiing, canoeing, windsurfing and, perhaps the most spectacular of all, white-water rafting. Rowing takes place on a straight course that's $1\frac{1}{4}$ miles long, with grandstands and scoreboards for official competitions. However, the most enthralling feature is the white-water slalom course. Water is diverted from the Trent at its higher level and channelled into a man-made rocky river, down which it tumbles and thrashes its spray-laden way to the lower level. Intrepid canoeists launch themselves down this torrent, though the ever-present ducks seem to think it a great deal of fuss about nothing. There are good views of the course from the grassy hillocks alongside, and a nearby control centre has changing rooms and equipment hire for anyone who wants to amuse the ducks.

Alongside the white-water course is the Trent, tranquil and wide with wooded hills forming a backdrop. A necklace of buoys strung across the river guards Holme sluice and guides boats towards the adjacent locks, the keeper deciding which chamber will be used depending on the size of the boat wishing to pass through. The Trent's system of traffic lights to signal lock-readiness to boat crews is easy to see here. Red means stop, the lock is set against you or is closed. Red and green together, the lock is being prepared for you but is not yet ready. Green, the lock is ready for you to enter. Amber means the keeper is not on duty and you may operate the lock yourself.

FROM SHARDLOW to Nottingham the Trent has been lined with various attractions; now it begins a quieter passage. Villages and towns are dotted along the Trent's banks, often these are the sites of the many ferries that used to cross the river; all are now gone, remembered only by faded picture postcards and pub names. With their demise, modern visitors have to rely on road bridges, a limited commodity with only six spanning the Trent's remaining eighty miles to the Humber. When planning an outing it is wise to note which bank you wish to visit—it can be a lengthy drive if you end up looking across the river at where you wish to be.

Typical of the smaller settlements along the Trent is Stoke Bardolph with the Ferry Boat Inn standing by the grass-banked river, the old ferry ramp still sloping down to the water. This section of the Trent is a designated jet ski area so weekends are enlivened or marred—probably an age-related difference of opinion—by the exciting roar or hideous screech of the small powered craft. In quieter times the Stoke Bardolph ferry crossed along a rope attached to pulleys on both banks, the wooden framework of which can be seen on the east bank at the end of a narrow lane.

Gunthorpe has the advantage of a bridge, a sturdy stone structure carrying the A6097. The Unicorn Hotel and two other pubs overlook the river, fronted by waterside parking, moorings for visiting craft, and summertime public boat trips. A few yards downstream, the Toll House restaurant stands high on the remains of the old bridge, replaced because it was too narrow for the volume of 1920s traffic. A short walk further on is Gunthorpe Lock, a good place to see boats passing through. Past the lock the path continues through meadows with shingle beaches, overlooked by a hilly and wooded far bank.

Hazelford Ferry, on the west bank near Bleasby, has a large pub with riverside tables, boats on moorings, and the old ferry slipway. Pleasant grassy riverside paths may be walked in both directions, the opposite bank still providing a wooded backdrop.

Centuries of floods caused most villages to develop on higher ground, delegating a solitary ferry-side pub to the risks of the riverbanks. Fiskerton is an exception. There's a car park at the downstream end of the village and from here a good grass-lined path goes between the river and a lovely selection of old houses, ending at the three-storeyed Bromley Arms and the old wharf. However, Fiskerton has a practical price to pay for this riverside location—the ever-present flood defences. The village perches on the edge of a wall with the Trent some feet down alongside. And, if the river should rise enough to top this, the houses all have walled gardens, the gateways incorporating steps to maintain the integrity of the defence against the river. At the wharf an old rusty gantry overlooks the Trent, formerly used to lift and lower items between the boatyard and vessels moored by the wall.

Between the villages the river passes through open fields, often rough grasslands that are allowed to flood when heavy rainfall swells the Trent. Near Farndon the main flow of the river goes over Averham Weir. It winds round via Kelham where the fields take excess waters away from Newark, the pleasant Nottinghamshire town which is on an ancient artificial cut and not the river proper. Perhaps it's the anomaly of Newark-on-Trent not actually being on the river of its name that creates the impression that the residents think little of the waterway in their midst. If that is so, it does not apply to the many visitors who stroll around Newark's comprehensive range of water-linked attractions—

a lock with the best public access for boat-watching, dry-docks, old warehouses, a pub-barge and boat trips.

Newark Castle

The A1 now bypasses the town and takes through-traffic away from the narrow streets, unlike the days when Newark's splendid five-arched stone bridge carried the Great North Road over the waterway. Now it's the crossing for the A6065 and a good central point with its large adjacent riverside car parks. The current bridge dates from the 1770s, but there has been a crossing here for many centuries, the Civil War battles for control of the bridge resulting in the ruin of the neighbouring castle. Many postcards feature the castle with boats passing beneath its walls, but 'wall' would be more accurate—behind the picturesque stonework is a grassy garden, a visitor centre and Tourist Information. In the words of the old music-hall song, this really is 'one of the ruins that Cromwell knocked about a bit'—but it looks good. Parallel to the river, and in front of the castle remains, is Castlegate. From this street various alleys and gateways wind through the old riverside buildings, many of which have been converted to craft workshops, exhibitions and housing. Foot-paths from here lead to the river and Newark Town lock with its good views of boating activity, guaranteed because the paths go over the lock-gates. The lock-keeper's control room overlooks the scene, high up with many windows so that approaching boats can be seen and the lock made ready for them—all indicated by the usual traffic light controls.

Next to the lock is a smaller chamber which is used as a dry-dock and for mooring the trip-boats in the winter. This is the original lock, but it was too small when cargo vessels used the river and it was replaced with the current chamber in 1952. On the west bank is a modern covered dry-dock and a British Waterways' yard. Various types of vessel may be seen in there for repair, the dry-dock providing a rare opportunity to see the hull shapes that give boats their stability. A waterside path leads back to the town bridge, the car parks, a floating pub-barge and trip-boats offering river cruises.

On the outskirts of Newark, boats pass through a second lock where the artificial cut through the town merges once more with the river proper. Six miles further downstream the Trent undergoes its major transformation—at Cromwell Lock it changes from a controlled river to a tidal inlet of the sea, almost a hundred miles from the coast. The lock itself is not easy to reach by road but the difference it makes to the river can be seen from the downstream banks. The villages stand further back and the intervening fields are more extensive and spanned by a flood bank. The A1133 runs parallel to the river on the eastern side, but this also keeps its distance.

Collingham has good cause to be wary of the Trent. The church at the top of Ferry Lane has the height of past floods marked in the stonework by the gate—1795, 1875, and 1947. Two miles away, at the bottom of the lane, the river innocently flows past an old wharf on the far bank, but there are clues that this is now an inlet of the sea: the most obvious are the tall black-and-white poles that mark the channel for boats if the river spreads over the fields. The international convention is that when heading upstream the poles topped with a 'cone' mark the right-hand side of the channel, those topped with a 'can' mark the left-hand side. The tidal rise here is very slight, but twice a day the river may be seen flowing in the opposite direction. As a result, boats on the remaining miles of the Trent time their journeys to cruise with the tide for as long as possible. Such vessels may include the barges that load with gravel from the huge riverside quarries at Girton, low-loaded they butt their way through the water.

A truthful picture of the river requires the inclusion of a feature less than scenic—a string of power stations—but as they are spaced out along ninety miles they hardly constitute an overwhelming problem. The power stations were built when coal was the main fuel for electricity generation and they were sited to take advantage of the nearby coalfields and the endless supply of cooling water in the Trent. After it has been used, the water is returned to the river rather warmer than when it left it. This sounds harmless enough—there's no danger of the Trent freezing in the winter—but it can cause 'thermal pollution' in the summer. This is when the overall temperature of the river becomes too high and it does the fish no good at all. However, this problem is now controlled and fish mortalities are rare. Now, as coal is phased out, some of the Trent's power stations are closing and gas-fired replacements are being built.

Opportunities to cross the river are now rare, the next being at Dunham Bridge, seventeen miles downstream from Newark and carrying the A57.[3] There are quiet walks along the east bank, especially upstream where a wooded ridge forms a backdrop. The road access means this is a popular stretch with anglers, the Trent being a premier coarse fishery.

Four miles further on the river arrives at another waterway junction—Torksey, where boats can divert into the Fossdyke, a canal built by the Romans to link Lindum (Lincoln) with the River Trisantona (Trent). The often busy lock into the Fossdyke is by the A156, with a car park, toilets and a restaurant.[4] Another ten miles and the Trent reaches Gainsborough, the town wholly on the Lincolnshire east bank and linked by its bridge to the Nottinghamshire west bank. Once a busy river-trading port, Gainsborough now ignores its history, the Trent hidden behind the old warehouses that used to be the centre of activity. However, new flood defences are planned for the town and they will include a riverside walkway and the regeneration of the old buildings; by the year 2000 things should look better.

Sea-going ships used to come this far upriver and goods were transhipped, via Gainsborough's warehouses, into smaller craft to go further upriver, but such activity has now ceased. However, sea-going ships of a maximum length of 190 feet still come this far up the Trent, about 60–70 each year, but they tie up at Beckingham Wharf on the opposite bank—Nottinghamshire's only sea-port. This wharf has a claim to being Britain's furthest inland port—eighty miles from the sea. Many foreign flags may be seen on the ships, as well as the Red Ensign, they carry varied cargoes including timber, rock salt and nitrates. The ships use the spring tides and have a pilot on board for the river passage.

The bridge at Gainsborough is a deciding point. If the rest of the river is to be explored, a bank needs to be selected: the next road bridge is eighteen miles away at Keadby. Both banks have secondary roads running parallel to the river, the high floodbanks allowing them to accompany the Trent safely on the rest of its journey to the Humber. The western side is usually chosen, the lock, and boats at West Stockwith attracting many visitors. This is where the Chesterfield Canal meets the Trent, and on the sheltered waters beyond the lock, a basin contains moorings for a mixture of river and canal craft. In West Stockwith village

3. *This is a toll-bridge: the payment for a car at the time of writing is 15p. Pedestrians have free passage.*
4. *Torksey Lock in included in the 'Fossdyke' chapter.*

Entrance to the Chesterfield Canal at West Stockwith

the Trent is joined by its last major tributary, the River Idle; the junction of the two rivers also marked as the northern end of the 84-mile Trent Valley Way footpath.[5]

After West Stockwith the Trent flows through vast acres of rich farmland with the occasional village peeping over the floodbanks and walls. Centuries ago the river used to spread over this flat area creating a marsh of little use to anyone. Many drainage schemes have reclaimed the land, and the towers of some of the windmills that used to pump the water into drainage ditches can still be seen. In the midst of this agricultural area is Keadby, its wharves, storage tanks and light industry clustered around the entrance to the Stainforth & Keadby Canal, the water route to Doncaster, Sheffield and Leeds. Keadby is the last crossing point on the Trent; a modern motorway bridge carries the M180 across, but the A18 uses a far more interesting structure. Carrying road and rail, Keadby bridge was built in 1916 and the eastern span used to lift to allow sailing ships with their tall masts to pass through. It does not open any more, but its design, a rolling bascule to be precise, was so advanced that the Science Museum in London still has a model of it on display. Wharves line both banks and ships up to 300 feet in length call to discharge and load cargoes—coal, bulk liquids, special steels, alloys, animal feed, coke and reels of paper. Near the bridge Gunness Wharf often has Norwegian ships alongside.

Three miles downstream the few houses of Amcotts look across to Flixborough Wharf on the east bank. Vessels sail from here each Friday, arrive at Antwerp on Monday, leave there on Tuesday and arrive back

5. *West Stockwith is covered in the 'Chesterfield Canal' and 'River Idle' chapters.*

A wharf at Keadby

at Flixborough on Thursday. Burton Stather, another three miles further on, is the Trent's last wharf and caters for ships carrying timber and tin plate from Sweden.

Yet another three miles and the river finally ends its 170-mile course at Trent Falls where the navigational Apex Light marks the merging of the Trent and Ouse and the creation of the Humber. It's a lonely, mud-surrounded, windswept spot, the roads having already veered away to more populated areas. The speed of the incoming tides can reach six knots, and when channelled into the Trent can create a tidal bore like the one on the River Severn. On the Trent it's called the 'Aegre' and if the conditions are right it is a considerable force to beyond West Stock-with. A free annual Aegre timetable is published by the NRA, but the wave is dependent on tide heights, wind direction and the amount of freshwater coming down the river so, as with most natural phenomena, nothing can be guaranteed.

With its international shipping, tidal waves, and gravel barges, it's sometimes difficult to remember that this is the same river that gives so much pleasure to leisure in Nottingham and Newark, fills marinas and lakes at Sawley and Colwick, suffers jet-skis at Stoke Bardolph, and provides miles of waterside walks and numerous waterside pubs. One of Britain's premier waterways—the River Trent.

Further Reading

Davy, Sam, *Nottinghamshire Rivers* (Ashbracken, 1991; ISBN 1-872356-05-2).
Hadfield, Charles, *The Canals of the East Midlands* (David & Charles). History.
Lund, Brian, *The River Trent: Reflections of a Bygone Age* (1993;
    ISBN 0-946245-67-3). Old picture postcards.
Aegre Timetable (Free, from the National Rivers Authority, as below).

Useful Contacts

British Waterways Managers responsible for:
    Derwent Mouth to Beeston Lock. Tel: 0115 9461017.
    Meadow Lane Lock to Gainsborough. Tel: 01636 705584.
Inland Waterways Association Tel: 0115 9875475.
Trent & Mersey Canal Society 34 Kennedy Avenue, New Sawley, Long Eaton,
    Nottingham NG10 3GF.
National Rivers Authority Tel: 0121 7112324.

Boat Trips/Hire-Boats

Forest Narrowboats Narrowboat hire, including by the day. Sawley.
    Tel: 0115 946 1539.
Trent Cruising *Trent Lady* cruises from Trent Bridge to Gunthorpe, up to 72
    diners, buffet, special functions, etc. Tel: 01850 774298.
Gunthorpe From outside Unicorn Hotel. Tel: 01636 704902.
Newark Newark Line. Tel: 01636 706479.

Public Transport

Rail Stations (Nearest*) Long Eaton, Attenborough*, Nottingham, Newark*,
    Gainsborough, Althorpe*.
Bus Information Tel: 0115 982 4268.

Places to Visit in the Area

Tourist Information Nottingham. Tel: 0115 947 0661.

Newark. Tel: 01636 78962.

Gainsborough. Tel: 01427 615411.

Holme Pierrepont, National Watersports Centre Nottingham. Varied water activities, especially white-water canoeing and rafting. No swimming. Tel: 0115 982 1212.

Cycle Hire and circular routes. Free leaflets. Tel: 0115 977 4483.

Circular Walks in Cranfleet Cut area. Leaflet No.16 (*The Cranfleet Trail*) is specially designed for disabled access. Tel: 0115 946 1321.

Trent Valley Way is 84 miles long. Also circular walks along it. Booklets from 0115 977 4483.

Newark Air Museum Tel: 01636 707170.

Gainsborough Model Railway Society Extensive model railway, east coast main line, runs to timetable. Contact for public viewing days. Tel: 01652 654657.

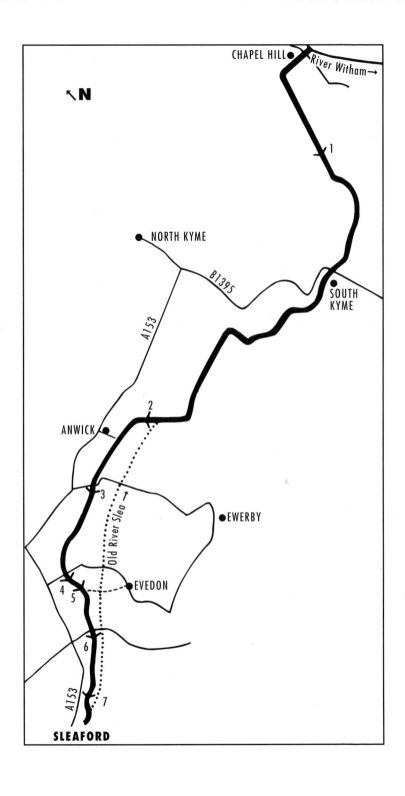

The Sleaford Navigation

Being restored; 13 miles long; 7 wide locks
Navigable for 8 miles from River Witham
OS map: Landranger sheets 130, 122
(also two very small sections on sheet 121)

'**C**OBBLERS'! it says in large letters on car windows in central Lincoln-shire. Is this a traditional fenlanders' welcome to visitors? No—on closer inspection the signs actually say 'Sleaford Navigation Society restoring from COBBLERS lock to Haverholme'. Dedicated to seeing boats again in Sleaford, the Society is working its way up from the River Witham; over half of the distance is now navigable and one target is the re-opening of Cobblers lock, the reason for the memorable slogan.

The source of the River Slea is north of Grantham, near the start of the A153. The river and the road then take much the same route: through Ancaster and Sleaford, north-east through the fertile fields of the Lincoln-shire countryside, eventually reaching the River Witham, and the national waterways system, near Tattershall.

Before reaching Sleaford, the river is unremarkable, indistinguishable from many others in Lincolnshire where almost every drop of water is regulated and land drainage is so important. This is a significant matter as the level in the Slea is controlled by the National Rivers Authority (NRA) and visitors may be disappointed if rainfall has been sparse; during the dry years in the late 1980s the Slea almost disappeared and the NRA listed it as one of this country's ten driest rivers. In normal conditions the Slea flows along and the NRA has installed various schemes to try to stop the water supply fluctuating between extremes.

Beyond Sleaford the river becomes the Sleaford Navigation and has for many centuries transported the trade, and driven the mills, of local merchants. It is a typical fenland waterway: flood-retaining banks on both sides, a towpath on the bank top allowing easy walking through a rural and peaceful landscape, and many access points by quiet country roads. Chapel Hill, where the Slea meets the Witham, and South Kyme are the only villages on the Navigation. Some people consider the Slea to be most attractive between Sleaford and Cobblers Lock; others value the peace and large skies of the fenland from Cobblers Lock to the Witham.

A GOOD PLACE to start a visit is the small market town of Sleaford, for centuries the commercial centre of the surrounding fenlands. On the eastern edge is Cogglesford Mill and lock—on the A153 with a good car park—from here it's a pleasant walk upstream into the town centre, half a mile along the towpath on the far bank.

Most of the locks on the Slea had a mill alongside powered by the change in river level; here the mill has not only survived it is being renovated to working condition. The present Cogglesford Mill dates from the eighteenth century and was last used in 1885; it then stood empty and neglected until 1990 when it was given to the District Council and restoration of the building and its machinery began. Now open to the public, admission is free and guided tours can be arranged. Alongside the mill is the top lock of the seven that climb up from the Witham; still derelict and awaiting the attention of the Navigation Society, its sides are still in position, but where the top and bottom gates should be is marked only by grooves in the walls.

Having said the Slea flows through Sleaford to the River Witham, inspection of a map will show that the story is a little more involved. On the towpath walk into Sleaford, outside the swimming baths to be precise, the Slea divides into two branches—known as the Old River and, what else, the New River. The Old River drops down over a weir to make its insignificant, but natural, way to just below Cobblers Lock. It's the New River that has the mills and locks and is known as the Sleaford Navigation, a label that bypasses the question of whether the waterway is a river or a canal. It may be that the Old River is the natural course of the Slea and the 'New River' a misnomer for a man-made channel, but if it is artificial it was done a long time ago and there is no evidence either way. What is known is that in the eighteenth century Sleaford merchants wanted cargo-carrying boats to reach their town and they used the easy option of adding locks to the New River, rather than digging a completely new canal.

SLEAFORD TOWN CENTRE

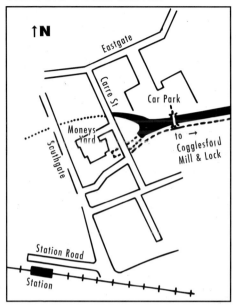

A little further along, the Navigation divides into two arms, both passing under Carre Street which in its heyday was Sleaford's busy industrial centre. One of the arms is now grassed over, but its route is still obvious. Along Carre Street is Money's Yard where boats could reach the windmill that still stands in the centre. The Tourist Information centre is in the mill tower and there are toilets and a coffee shop in the Yard. A little further along Carre Street an old doorway has a stone portal with the inscription 'Navigation Wharf 1792', but it was probably moved to its present site at a later date.

Trade on the waterway was controlled by the Sleaford Navigation Company and its stone-built office building can still be seen in a private yard off the eastern side of Carre Street. Built in 1838, and bearing the company's arms over the door, it is thought to be a unique memorial of the canal age, the only canal company office building of that era to have survived. Sadly, it is neglected and deteriorating.

FROM SLEAFORD the towpath can be walked all the way to the junction with the River Witham at Chapel Hill; it is wide and kept mown, but can be hummocky and ankles may appreciate the support of good walking shoes. Waterways such as the Slea are very much a question of taste: featureless, boring with a few derelict locks—or the means of access to miles of secluded countryside that lift the spirit and the mind.

Entrance to the Canal Company offices,
with the Company seal above the door

Timing may have an influence on the verdict: the countryside is not so secluded at harvest time when the combines are hoovering the fields; nor is it peaceful when the RAF is flying on weekdays from its many Lincolnshire airfields. On a fine early Saturday morning however, when the distant traffic is charging towards Skegness and the fields and skies are unpeopled, the Sleaford Navigation can be a gentle, timeless place of simple pleasure.

Paper Mill Lock, by the Evedon road off the A153, is an easily-accessible spot for enjoying the peaceful countryside, there is hardly any traffic on the lane and the wheatfields spread for miles around with tree-topped ridges marking the horizon. At the moment, the Slea makes a pleasant noise as it flows uncontrolled down through the lock, making the most of its freedom before an orderly state is imposed by the Navigation Society's restoration work. On the far side was Evedon Paper Mill where, until it was demolished in the 1930s, seven sets of millstones made paper for a Boston printing works. From Paper Mill Lock to Corn Mill Lock, only a quarter of a mile upstream, is a pleasant walk where the mill buildings have survived in the grounds of a private house. In the summer roses grow over the edge of the lock chamber and swallows swoop overhead, many of them probably nesting in Holdingham Mill, the long red building, where flour was produced until 1957. In the garden is a delightful feature—an octagonal tollbooth where the navigation company's collector gathered payments from the boats using the waterway.[1]

There is no road access to the infamous Cobblers Lock, but if you wish to see the restoration work that has been done it can most easily be reached from Anwick village: off the A153, drive to the bottom of River Lane, and walk left along the towpath for one mile. The river is shallow and slow flowing, the far bank is wooded, and beyond the towpath the Lincolnshire prairies ripple to the horizon. The waterbirds are not used to being disturbed—a sudden whir of wings betraying their presence; on the towpath pheasants and partridges run from cover into the fields. Below the lock the Old River flows in, having taken its own course from Sleaford. The area is not scenically attractive in the conventional tourist brochure way, but the solitude of sitting quietly at Cobblers Lock is wonderful: a variety of sounds can be heard—soft

Near South Kyme

1. *There is no public road access to Corn Mill Lock from the A153.*

A boat festival at South Kyme

South Kyme

scufflings and splashings, a cock pheasant croaking, dragonflies buzzing, the water running over the lock weir; and there is the chance that a boat may appear as the Slea is navigable from here.

The remaining miles of the Sleaford Navigation are the same, if anything becoming more remote as the waterway reaches deeper into the fens, only its passage through the village of South Kyme changing the scene.

At Chapel Hill the Slea adds its waters to one of fenland's major rivers—the Witham, flowing from Grantham and Lincoln, to Boston and The Wash. The main road through the village crosses the Slea a few yards from the junction of the rivers, the stone balustrade of the bridge showing the border between the two Lincolnshire areas of North

Kesteven and Holland. On the Slea, just upstream of the road bridge, is a structure that looks like a lock but is in fact a flood-gate which is left open when water levels are normal. The better towpath to the Witham is on the North Kesteven bank, past the moored boats to a wide impressive river where the air is cool and refreshing. After the narrow, shallow Navigation, the Witham looks like the Mississippi rolling down to the sea, but it is controlled just as much as the little Slea—wayward water is not tolerated in Lincolnshire.

Further Reading

Hadfield, Charles, *The Canals of Eastern England* (David & Charles). History.
Robinson, David N., *Lincolnshire Boats and Bridges in Camera* (Quotes Ltd, 1989; ISBN 0-86023-365-0). Old photographs.

Useful Contacts

Sleaford Navigation Society 8 Kirkby Close, Southwell, Notts. Tel: 01636 812572.
National Rivers Authority, Lincoln. Tel: 01522 513100.

Public Transport

Rail Station Sleaford.

Places to Visit in the Area

Tourist Information Sleaford. Tel: 01529 414294.
Aviation History There are many RAF bases in the area, past and present, including the Battle of Britain Memorial Flight of Spitfires, Hurricanes and a Lancaster bomber. There are many free leaflets available from Sleaford Tourist Information, the most informative covers the North Kesteven Airfield Trail.
Billinghay Animal Centre and Children's Farm North Kyme. On the A153, nine miles north east of Sleaford. Children can meet and learn about farm animals and rare breeds. Tel: 0526 860305.
Heckington Windmill Working, wind permitting. Open on Sundays all year, other days in summer. Tel: 01529 60765.

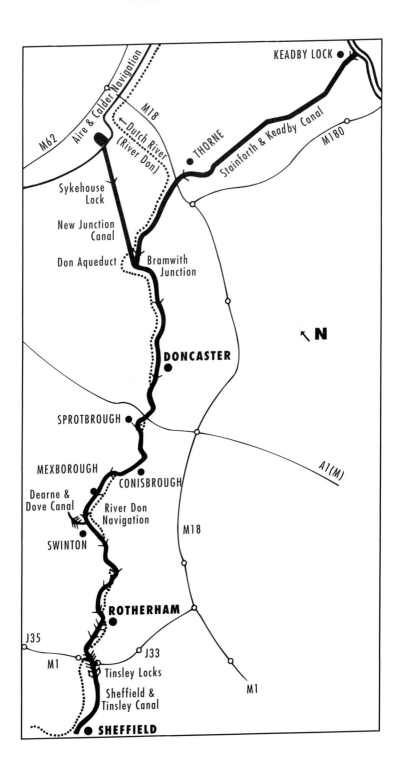

The Sheffield & South Yorkshire Navigation

Navigable; 48 miles long
28 wide locks
OS map: Landranger sheets 111, 112

IT HAS a grand name—The Sheffield & South Yorkshire Navigation—and it provides a grand selection of waterway sights. At Bramwith boats cross above the River Don on a unique aqueduct and a nearby swing-bridge moves the road aside for boats to pass. At Keadby the navigation meets the tidal River Trent and sea-going ships unload. And at Sheffield new moorings adjoin two spectacular sports stadiums, the innovative Super-tram system provides return transport for towpath walkers, and in the city centre, the terminus basin re-opened in 1995 as the renovated Victoria Quays.

The title 'Sheffield & South Yorkshire Navigation' (SSYN) is an overall term for four separate waterways that were built to provide transport for the expanding industries of Sheffield, Rotherham and Doncaster. Two of the four—the New Junction Canal and the Don Navigation—were modernised in the 1980s and are used by large vessels carrying cargoes to Doncaster and Rotherham; the locks are cavernous, and sharp bends on the water-way have been alleviated. The other two components of the SSYN—the Sheffield & Tinsley Canal and the Stainforth & Keadby Canal—were not modernised and their smaller locks are used mainly by pleasure craft.

The SSYN's diverse nature is a result of this history, and a route that links a city centre to quiet countryside.

The Sheffield & Tinsley Canal

CADMAN Street is a useful place to start a visit to the Sheffield & Tinsley Canal. An easy one-hour walk will discover a multitude of sights—some old, some very new—the option of a return ride on Supertram, and the circle completed via the restored canal terminus basin.

A city-centre canal is perhaps not an immediately appealing place to visit, especially when the city's name is synonymous with heavy industry, but what remains of Sheffield's steel heartland is along the higher reaches of the River Don, not the canal. That may seem a moot point when you arrive at Bridge No. 3 (Cadman St) to find a waterway tucked between metallurgical laboratories, a gas-holder, the boldly-named Sipelia Works and a motley collection of workshops. This is however Sheffield's major body of still water, the gross pollution of water, air and land is now in the past, and wild flowers, butterflies, birds, dragonflies and water mammals have all found this corridor through an area otherwise barren for them. Even in a city a canal provides a quiet, little-known way of bypassing the hassle and noise of modern life.[1]

I think Saturday mornings are the best time to explore urban waterways. In Sheffield the shopping crowds are milling into the markets and stores, and the roads are busy with a steady stream of traffic. Down by the canal there is another world: some overtime is being earned in the adjacent works—a radio plays near an open window, a fussy fork-lift bleats a warning, a drop-hammer laboriously thumps, voices echo from cavernous works, drills drill, rollers roll, and the smell of hot metal wafts from who knows where. What you see of all this apparent industrial activity is—nothing—only occasional figures popping in and out of doors like little boiler-suited weather indicators.

The bridges on this canal bear attractive plates with their name and number—counting from the city centre—and the date of construction. The Cadman Street (No. 3) bridge plate is marked '1819', the year the canal was completed, indicating that this is one of the only two remaining original bridges. The second is Bacon Lane (No. 6) Bridge, notorious in the days of the heavily-laden working boats, as the dimensions of its stone arch, 15 feet 6 inches wide and 10 feet high, have always determined the size of craft that can reach Sheffield basin. Often it was a very tight fit.

As a contrast, the Sheffield & Tinsley Canal also has three of the most attractive new bridges in the country—handsome black-and-white steel structures, two based on a design historically used on the Birmingham canals. The first is immediately after Pinfold Bridge (No. 7) and it carries

---

1. *Signs to the towpath are planned at the restored canal basin (Victoria Quays), but at the time of writing the construction work has not been completed.*

New bridges across the canal in Sheffield

the innovative Supertram system; the nearby second carries a cycleway. When the canal was built, excavating this section was a major task: substantial amounts of manpower were needed to dig a cutting 150 yards long and 36 feet deep. Luckily—for the canal company, that is—there were many men unemployed at that time because of the recession that followed the end of the Napoleonic Wars. The Overseers of the Poor were able to supply plenty of labour and as a result the excavation of the cutting was both quick and cheap.

The towpath is wide, even and well drained throughout this walk. Yes, there is some litter and graffiti, but this is an old part of an old city and unfortunately it is to be expected. If the eyes are offended, there is compensation for the ears—the songs of blackbird, wren and robin are vibrant. Uplifted eyes may also note that many of the buildings have evidence of past trade on the canal—bricked-up windows, doors and arches at the water's edge where boats once moored to load and unload. Bridge 9 has rope marks on its corners and there are new mooring pontoons in the adjacent basin.

After this bridge the canal bends to the left, the aspect opens out, and in the distance can be seen the modernistic yellow-gantried design of the Don Valley athletics stadium. Beyond that, Sheffield Arena, an indoor stadium used for pop concerts and the sell-out home matches of the Steelers ice-hockey team. Before reaching these products of the 1990s there is another of the canal's original 1819 structures: an aqueduct that takes the waterway over the Worksop Road. Approaching the stadiums, the banks have been landscaped; there are paved areas and seats, and pontoon moorings for visiting boats. Here the third new

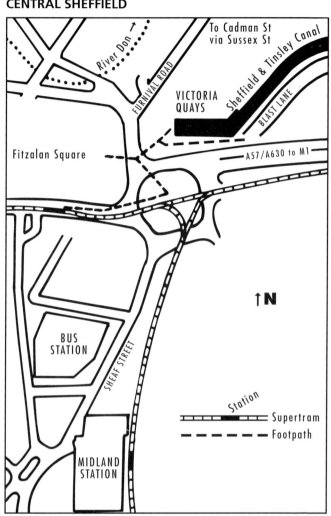

bridge—a small-scale replica of the famous one at Ironbridge in Shropshire—gives access to a canal-side Supertram stop for a return ride to Sheffield city centre.[2] From the stop at Fitzalan Square, walkways pass over the busy city traffic to the canal's terminus basin, a good view of which is seen from Supertram, now known as Victoria Quays.

2. *There are ticket machines at all Supertram stops. If you wish to take a longer walk, the towpath continues to the eleven locks of the Tinsley flight, taking the canal down to meet the River Don near the huge Meadowhall shopping complex. Another Supertram stop is accessible from between the third and fourth locks.*

As I write, the basin is undergoing extensive reconstruction. The old warehouses are being converted to offices, shops and cafés. The canal is once more to play a part in the life of Sheffield city centre, albeit rather different from the time when timber was unloaded and stored, grain was unshipped by a bucket elevator, and boats with various cargoes floated beneath the straddle warehouse. Cadman Street (No. 3) Bridge, where this visit began, is just beyond the basin.

Don Navigation

The Sheffield & Tinsley Canal ends at the bottom of the eleven locks that take the waterway down to the River Don. From here the Don is used to provide the major part of the SSYN, 25 miles through Rotherham and Doncaster. It is a typical river navigation, with weirs avoided by artificial cuts containing one or more locks. Because the river is used between these lock-cuts there is not a specific towpath on some sections. However, there is now a good path between Sheffield and Rotherham, with bus and train stations adjacent for the return journey. In 1994–95 Rotherham Council and British Waterways worked together to create a new towpath in the town which has solved the previous access problems.

Beyond Rotherham the locks are huge and power-operated. Unfortunately, the modernisation in the 1980s seems to have come too late as commercial use of the navigation is spasmodic, unused barges are moored at many locations. At Swinton the first three locks of the Dearne & Dove Canal are now used as a boatyard by Waddingtons. This is a family company doggedly convinced that carrying by water has a future, its moored and silent barges patiently wait for the upturn on the SSYN.[3]

Through Mexborough to Conisbrough, with its Norman castle on the hill, the Don Navigation continues with its river–canal mixture, hopefully it will have a continuous towpath in the future—perhaps as part of The Earth Centre, an environmental theme park planned for 1996. A gem that is already there is Sprotbrough, with its lock, wooded walks, water-bus, nature reserve, waterside car park, the Boat Inn, and a floating art gallery. The charming village is higher up the hillside, but most visitors descend to the valley bottom, to the magnetic lure of water, boats and bread-hungry ducks. The river falls over a wide weir and the boats are moored on the adjacent artificial cut to the lock, including *Sprotbro' Painter*, the narrowboat gallery of waterway artist Sheila Bury. Nearby may be *Wyre Lady*—the water-bus used on summer Sundays and Bank Holidays—a fine old vessel with a history that includes taking supplies to the liners *Queen Mary* and *Queen Elizabeth* when they were

3. *This area is covered in more detail in the 'Dearne & Dove Canal' chapter.*

troopships in World War II. She is owned by Alan Oliver, as are the barges and workboats that may also be present.

The upstream towpath passes between the river and Sprotbrough Flash, a large lake which is a nature reserve administered by the Yorkshire Wildlife Trust. From the towpath the lake is masked by trees, but there are two places where a path leads to well-equipped bird-watching hides overlooking the Flash. In this area, especially in the spring, you are certainly in the minority if you haven't a pair of binoculars around your neck. The path continues to the end of the lake, a circular walk possible by following it up the hillside and back through the woods to the car park area. Downstream the towpath passes the lock and then along a tree-canopied stretch, until the hum of the traffic on the A1 intrudes as the road passes high above the river. Many people stroll back the way they came, others climb the steps by the road bridge and walk via the village, down Boat Lane by the church, and back to the riverside area.

In the centre of Doncaster the River Don is left for the last time, and from here the rest of the SSYN is all man-made canals. The lower reaches of the Don used to be navigable many centuries ago, but the building of the SSYN's canals provided an easier water route and eventually the river was used no more.[4] Sheffield's river now flows into the River Ouse near Goole, changed from its original route by the seventeenth-century Dutch engineers who drained the great flood plains between the Ouse and the Trent. This is also the reason for the Don's bewildering change of name; for the last few miles of its course it is known as the Dutch River. The Don Navigation is sometimes shown, especially on Ordnance Survey maps, as the River Dun Navigation—historically correct, but confusing. Now you can see why British Waterways prefer to call the whole navigable system here the SSYN, also historically correct!

Whatever it's called, Doncaster is trying to improve the canal through the town, as is Rotherham, and various schemes are transforming the old commercial waterway into a pleasant feature, although much remains to be done. Both towns are changing away from heavy industry, but the transformation has been painful and the SSYN must take its place among the many projects planned. One example is Doncaster's canal-side power station: once supplied with coal by boat, it has been demolished and replaced with a new prison on the semi-island between the river and the canal—known locally as 'Doncatraz'. Strict warning signs prohibit mooring nearby—no boat-borne escapes from the 'island'!

The Don Navigation ends at Bramwith Junction where boats, and towpath walkers, have a choice of routes along the two remaining waterways

---

4. To be historically accurate , the present 'canal' beyond Doncaster is the river improved beyond recognition. The present 'river' is an artificial channel. Confusion is common!

of the SSYN: along the New Junction Canal to the Aire & Calder Navigation, the River Ouse and the northern waterways; or east along the Stainforth & Keadby Canal to the River Trent and the Midlands and Lincolnshire.

Bramwith Junction

Junction 4 of the M18 gives easy road access to South Bramwith and Kirk Bramwith: small, quiet villages in an area laced with waterways. The two canals—the New Junction and the Stainforth & Keadby—are crossed in this area by a succession of moveable bridges, some lift, others swing. Children love to watch the rigmarole when a boat comes along: klaxons sound, barriers descend across the road, the bridge lifts or swings, the boat passes through, the bridge returns to its original position, more klaxons, the barriers rise. It is fascinating and it's not unknown for children-filled cars to spend a pleasant summer Sunday driving from one bridge to another to see the road move. For watchers of such activities, the swing-bridge near Kirk Bramwith has the advantage of being on the New Junction, a straight canal where the approach of an entertaining boat can be spotted when the distant lift-bridges rise and fall. Each bridge on the Stainforth & Keadby Canal was, until quite recently, operated by a resident keeper. Now, apart from the road and rail bridges at Keadby, they have been converted to self-operation by boat crews, the control panels activated by a special British Waterways' key.

By South Bramwith's swing-bridge a track-road leads down to the lock with its pristine white-painted keeper's house, and a network of walks by the two canals and the River Don. Many boats are usually moored nearby, especially on summer weekends when members of the deliciously-named Strawberry Island Boat Club often cruise down from Doncaster.

The lock itself is interesting because it has three sets of gates instead of the usual two. The extra set was installed to make the lock longer for coal-carrying commercial craft, a traffic that ceased but, if the trial run in 1994 was successful, coal may once again pass this way from Hatfield Colliery to Ferrybridge Power Station.

Past the lock the canal-side can be followed to the wide waters of Bramwith Junction—turn left to Sheffield, turn right onto the New Junction Canal and the waterways beyond to Goole, Leeds and York. Large commercial vessels pass here, but they no longer carry fuel for the looming power station, because Thorpe Marsh closed down in early 1994. It is due to be demolished in 1995 and that will change the skyline here; the cooling towers are (were) a landmark for the whole length of the straight New Junction Canal.

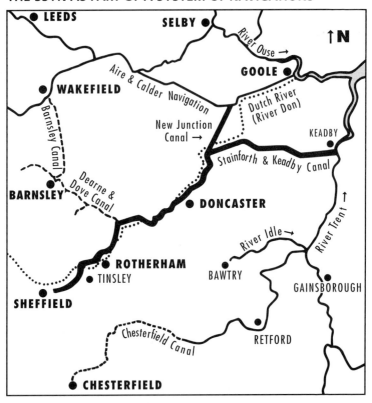

From here a short walk along the New Junction will find one of this country's most unusual waterway structures—the Don Aqueduct. Via this sturdy edifice, boats on the canal cross over the River Don, their bow waves cascading down to the river over the unprotected side. At each end is a large guillotine gate, normally kept raised, but when lowered they protect the canal and the surrounding area if the river reaches flood levels. This may look unlikely, but the Don is tidal here and higher than usual spring tides, topped by excessive amounts of freshwater coming down the river, combined with an on-shore wind in the Humber Estuary can bring the water levels close to the top of the enclosing floodbanks.

Paths lead along the bank tops, and it's a short walk across the intervening land back to the lock. From Bramwith the two canals gradually diverge, the New Junction following its straight course through Sykehouse Lock to Southfield Junction where it meets the Aire & Calder Navigation. The Stainforth & Keadby turns more eastward and passes through Thorne

A typical lift-bridge on the New Junction Canal

Thorne Lock

where there is another lock. This small town is another example of progress: it was once a busy port and boat-building centre on the River Don known as Thorne Quay until the water trade moved to the new canal. Then the river's route was altered, and later the M18 divided the old and new parts of the town. Now, the old port area is known as Waterside and little remains, not even the river, only the bed it used to flow in.

Via umpteen swing bridges the canal eventually reaches the River Trent at one of its name towns, Keadby—one of those places that are

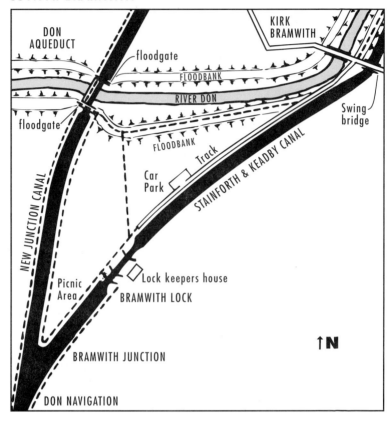

admittedly an acquired taste, but it can be worthwhile taking a sip. OK, so the canal area of Keadby looks a little scruffy. At first sight, it's tempting to drive on to somewhere more eye-pleasing, somewhere more 'touristy', but it's a working inland port, and such locations are not known for their superficial glamour. If however, the sight of the road swinging back to allow boats to pass, a railway line doing the same thing, sea-going ships unloading and pleasure craft passing through a lock sound interesting, then stop and give Keadby a little of your time. Above all, you will find the people friendly, helpful and unhurried—a priceless attribute for any place. Evenings in the canal-side Friendly Fox pub are—so I'm told—a congenial way to meet a unique mix of sailors of all types! There are few pubs where you can find pleasure-boating families, river-barge crews, and from the sea-going ships Scandinavians, Russians, Germans and Dutch.

A canal-side car park gives good access to the towpath, usually lined with moored craft, their crews pottering about.[5] Keadby Lock is the link between the canal and the River Trent. There are keepers on duty most of the time but because the river is tidal, the lock is only operational at certain times around High Water.

The river wharves are either side of the canal's entrance and ships unloading leave little room for boats using the lock to pass between them. From the river, crews not familiar with Keadby anxiously scan the banks, the lock's location often unclear from their point of view. Once safely into the entrance, visitors find a lock with four sets of gates instead of two, an arrangement that allows craft to pass through when the Trent rises to a higher level than the canal.[6]

A taste of what is to come for visiting boaters is the swing-bridge immediately outside the lock. Operated by the keepers, it is much more substantial than the lane-carrying bridges further along the canal. Beyond, the Stainforth & Keadby Canal stretches wide and straight into the distance. In earlier times, this water would have been filled with keels and barges, some with engines, others with sails, taking cargoes to and from the Yorkshire industrial centres—Rotherham, Doncaster and Sheffield. Now it's quiet, with only the clanging of the riverside cranes creating echoes of past commercial activity.

Change cannot be halted however, and obvious proof of this is the new industrial complex a little further along the canal, on the far bank. This is one of the new gas-fired power stations, part of the controversial 'dash for gas' that has closed so many collieries and taken coal traffic from the waterways. It was completed in 1994, the same year that saw the closure of Thorpe Marsh Power Station, near Bramwith Junction, and the cessation of its water-borne fuel service.

In the distance a railway signal box can be seen, high above the waterway. If you fancy a walk along the scrubby-edged towpath, the surface a little uneven, you will find that the signalman operates a Meccanolike movable railway bridge. **The towpath crosses the railway at track level, so please be careful**. Figuring out how this structure moves without seeing it do so is a challenge to the practical-minded. Those of us who look bemused at this complex mixture of aged timber and latticed grey riveted steel, are best timing their walk to coincide with the arrival of a boat, and watching. A blast of boat-horn tells the signalman that passage is required and eventually, sometimes three or four trains later, this unusual bridge retracts onto its abutments and the boat cruises through—only to stop again to operate the first of the many crew-operated

5. The car park entrance is an unmarked private road immediately before the lights/barriers on the south side of the swing-bridge. The road runs alongside the canal and ends at the car park.
6. Page 15 has a diagram of such a lock.

swing-bridges along this canal. This is not a waterway for boaters in a hurry.

Standing at Keadby, it is difficult to believe that this is part of the same system as the canal basin in Sheffield's city centre, but it is: one segment of the varied waterways that make up the Sheffield & South Yorkshire Navigation—the SSYN.

Further Reading

Richardson, Christine, and John Lower, *The Complete Guide to the Sheffield & South Yorkshire Navigation* (Sheffield: The Hallamshire Press, 1995; ISBN I-8747-18-07-5; £6.95). Detailed pocket-sized guide, includes navigational information.

Hadfield, Charles, *The Canals of Yorkshire and North East England* (David & Charles). History.

Taylor, Mike, *Memories of the Sheffield and South Yorkshire Navigation* (Yorkshire Waterway Publications, 1988).

Willan, T.S., *The Early History of the Don Navigation* (USA: Augustus M. Kelley, 1968).

Useful Contacts

British Waterways Manager responsible for the navigation. Tel: 01636 705584.
Inland Waterways Association Tel: 01302 873127.

Boat Trips/Hire-Boats

Sheffield Canal Company Sussex Street. Tel: 0114 272 7233.
Alan Oliver (Cruises) Ltd Sprotbrough. Cruises and water-bus service. Tel: 01302 856513.
Ashnidd Boat Company Bramwith. Group cruises on *Ashanti Gold*. Tel: 0860 866843.
Yorkshire Rose Marina Unit 9, Leach Lane, Mexborough S64 0EN. Tel: 01709 571555. Boat for hire.

Angling (Main clubs, page 207)

Sheffield & Tinsley Canal First-class canal fishery. Roach, perch, carp, gudgeon.
River Don (Tinsley to Sprotbrough) Poorer water quality means fishing is patchy, some areas satisfactory, others poor. Roach, perch, some carp.
River Don (downstream of Sprotbrough), New Junction Canal, Stainforth & Keadby Canal Very good fishing, heavily used for contests, e.g. the 1994 National Championships. Roach, chub, gudgeon, bream.

Public Transport

Rail Stations (Nearest*) Sheffield, Meadowhall, Rotherham Central*, Swinton,
  Mexborough*, Doncaster, Kirk Sandall, Thorne South*, Crowle*,
  Althorpe.
Supertram Sheffield. Information Line: 0114 276 8688.

Places to Visit in the Area

Tourist Information Sheffield. Tel: 0114 273 4671.
  Rotherham. Tel: 01709 823611.
  Doncaster. Tel: 01302 734309.
Five Weirs Walk, Sheffield. Details from Sheffield Tourist Information.
Sprotbro' Painter Sheila Bury, Sprotbrough. Tel: 01302 856902.
Sprotbrough Flash Yorkshire Wildlife Trust, 10 Toft Green, York YO1 1JT.
  Tel: 01904 659570.
Conisbrough Castle English Heritage. Tel: 01709 863329.
The Earth Centre Conisbrough. First phase opening 1995.
  Details from Doncaster Tourist Information.

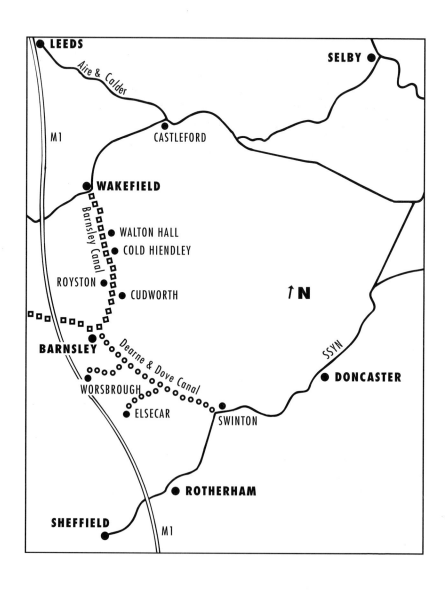

LEEDS

SELBY

Aire & Calder

M1

CASTLEFORD

WAKEFIELD

Barnsley Canal

WALTON HALL

COLD HIENDLEY

ROYSTON

CUDWORTH

↑N

BARNSLEY

Dearne & Dove Canal

SSYN

DONCASTER

WORSBROUGH

ELSECAR

SWINTON

ROTHERHAM

SHEFFIELD

M1

The Barnsley Canal
and The Dearne
& Dove Canal

Both canals are unnavigable
Barnsley Canal, 16 miles, 20 wide locks
Dearne & Dove Canal (main line) 10 miles, 19 locks
Elsecar Branch, 2 miles, 6 locks
Worsbrough Branch, 2 miles, 0 locks
OS map: Landranger sheet 111

THE Barnsley, and the Dearne & Dove: two canals—always rivals but
united by geography, history and plans for the future. The rich Barnsley
coal seam was the lure for both waterways, it was the source of their
success—and the resultant mining subsidence was the cause of their even-
tual closure.

*Exploring derelict canals is an acquired taste: for the connoisseur perhaps,
or those with a Livingstonian compulsion to follow a waterway upstream
to discover its source. Why are there mooring-rings in B&Q's car park?
Why is a small footbridge carried over the River Dearne on four massive
stone pillars? Exploration of these two canals will also find Worsbrough
Country Park, Elsecar's heritage workshops, reservoir fishing, quiet countryside walks—and pulley stones.*

The Barnsley Canal

THE SIXTEEN miles of the Barnsley Canal once formed a 'J'-shaped
link between the town and the Aire & Calder Navigation at Wakefield.
Much of the waterway can still be found, and approximately half of it
contains water even if the locks have been filled in. Fifteen of those

The Barnsley Canal near Walton Hall

locks are on the first stretch, the climb out of the River Aire's valley. The top lock of the flight brings the canal to the level it keeps for the next eleven miles, a major engineering achievement in such a hilly area.

From Walton Hall the canal is a popular walking route, although the standard rule of exploring derelict canals does apply—winter is best if you want to see much of the waterway because the summer vegetation grows high and luxuriant. However, the path itself is good and the many tracks through Haw Park make a pleasant four-mile circular route back.[1]

It is quiet here, peaceful enough to appreciate the two bridges, originals, built with the canal in the first years of the nineteenth century. One carries the road to Walton Hall, unnoticed by the people who drive over it. Down by the canal its ageless beauty can be appreciated, the stone-flagged towpath passing beneath the perfect arch, the man-made lines of the stonework disguised by draped foliage. As a reminder that its beauty was to accommodate working boats, the bridge corners bear the rope-groove evidence of their passing. A further sign of a practical

1. *There is a small car-parking area on the approach road to Walton Hall, where it crosses the canal.*

past is the wide vertical gap halfway through the span, made to take stop-planks when canal maintenance was required.

There is water in the canal here, which contains many reeds in the summer, creating a suitable habitat for waterbirds, and the towpath hedges are full of birdsong. Skirting the edge of Haw Park the Barnsley Canal enters Walton Cutting, the rock through which the navvies hacked the waterway, obvious as a sheer wall by the towpath.

At the southern corner of Haw Park is Cold Hiendley Reservoir, built to supply water to the canal as was Wintersett Reservoir beyond it, both are popular fishing waters. Unfortunately, necessary strengthening of Cold Hiendley's retaining bank has extended it, and for a short stretch it obliterates the canal it was built to serve. However, at the northern end of the bank, the towpath can be found by taking the left-hand path after crossing a footbridge. Within a few yards is a marvellous example of one of the Barnsley Canal's gems—a pulley stone. On tight bends the towrope between the horse and the boat would cut across at an angle, making life difficult for the boatman and the horse. The solution on this canal was to have a stone block on the bend, by the towpath. On top of the block was a pulley-wheel round which the towrope was placed, and as the horse rounded the sharp bend, the rope between it and the boat was kept at the correct angle.[2]

After the reservoir the canal continues to Notton Cutting, its wooded sides a beautiful sight in the autumn. From here it reaches the outskirts of Barnsley, passing between Royston and Cudworth. Armed with an OS map and booklets from the Barnsley Canal Group, the intrepid waterways explorer can follow the route by foot and car, but be careful, this can become addictive. Families have been seen searching out the smallest clues: a self-organised treasure hunt for Canal Street, The Keel Inn, Wharf Street. Which brings us to mooring-rings in B&Q's car park. Just north of the centre of Barnsley there is a very large roundabout on the A61, in the centre of which is a B&Q store. The long car park wall is built of immense stones into which the mooring-rings are set. It all makes sense when you realise that the cars are 'in the canal' and the wall was a wharf where the boats used to stop to load and unload. By looking across the road in a direct extension of the stone wall, a gap in the buildings can be seen and an information sign. This is the canal's route and the way to a waterside walk, the remains of a magnificent aqueduct and pleasant parkland along the valley of the River Dearne.

To find this part of the canal by car drive into Twibell Street, a minor exit off the B&Q roundabout on the A61. Second right is Eaming View, at the end of which is a car park that is actually on the line of the canal.

2. *Wakefield Council has canal restoration at Cold Hiendley in its 1995 programme.*

BARNSLEY

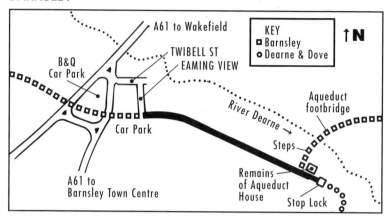

This can be proved by walking a few yards to the right, from where the B&Q mooring wall can be seen in a direct line from where you are standing. However, the major points are to the left. The Barnsley Canal is in good condition here: filled with water and ducks, and fringed with reeds and fishermen. The surfaced path runs alongside the canal and follows the edge of the River Dearne's wide valley, the land dropping away to playing fields and the tidy grassed acres of the Dearne Valley Country Park through which the river flows. It's easy to forget that this is the centre of Barnsley.

Eventually the canal widens for a few yards and it is easy to miss the significance of this area. From its start at Wakefield, the canal runs almost due south for over ten miles, until reaching Barnsley where it turns to the west to form the bottom bend of its 'J'-shaped route. To complete that turn, the Barnsley Canal had to cross the River Dearne and its valley. It did this on a magnificent five-arch aqueduct, one of the finest built by William Jessop, the eminent canal engineer.

Unfortunately, it had to be demolished when the canal became disused, because subsidence had caused the stone pillars to crack and they could not safely carry the heavy weight of the water in its trough. Steps from the path lead down to the remains of that aqueduct—a footbridge across the river supported on the original stone pillars, cracks and all.

Because the Barnsley Canal turned here to cross the valley, it is confusing to see a length of water carrying on in a straight line alongside the path. The explanation is that it's another canal: it's the Dearne & Dove coming up from the south, and this is the junction of the two waterways. A few yards along the Dearne & Dove is a derelict lock chamber, a stop-lock—the usual demarcation line between two canals. At the junction are two more pulley stones, but without their pulleys,

William Jessop's five-arch aqueduct at Barnsley

to help the boats make the tight turn to and from the aqueduct. Also the stone foundations of Aqueduct House, a cottage at the junction, have been preserved to complete a little-known collection of waterway heirlooms.

The Dearne & Dove Canal

Like an exotic dancer, the Dearne & Dove Canal has gems at its extremities. Unfortunately the similarity ends there because the waterway has precious little inbetween—a state of affairs not to the liking of the energetic volunteers of the Barnsley Canal Group who are striving to add more flesh to the skeleton.

The main line runs northward from the Don Navigation at Swinton near Rotherham, following the Dearne valley ten miles to Barnsley and the junction already described. On its way, two side-canals branch off: one to Worsbrough, the other to Elsecar. However, little of these routes can be seen, unless you have the exploratory zeal of some waterways enthusiasts who must find every nook and cranny of a disused canal. Those untouched by 'waterway fever' will probably prefer a visit to Worsbrough Country Park: 200 acres with footpaths, reservoir fishing, a working farm with animals, a mill museum, and special events on bank holidays.[3] The link with the Dearne & Dove is that the reservoir was created to supply water to the canal; the end of the Worsbrough Branch is nearby but only a few of the park's visitors find it because it's the other side of the A61. At the bottom of the overflow car park, a

---

3. *On the A61, two miles north of Junction 36 on the M1*

path to the left leads to the canal. A short stretch is in water and popular with fishermen, the surrounding neatly-mown grass makes it difficult to imagine the activity here in the canal's heyday. What is now the A61 was always an important turnpike road and this was a busy tranship-ment point between boats and waggons. The only sign now of such activity is the name of the nearby pub—The Wharf.

In the 1920s and '30s nearby Elsecar had the nickname 'Elsecar-by-the-Sea'. Crowds of people from the industrial towns who had never been to the coast used to flock to the village's park with its large reser-voir. Few knew, or cared, that this body of water was also built to supply the Dearne & Dove Canal, feeding supplies into the channel at the end of the Elsecar Branch. The reservoir is still there by the park, but it's now a quieter haven for fishermen and bird-watchers. Nearer to the village centre are the Heritage Workshops, a new project open now but due for completion in 1997. The complex is adjacent to the wharf at the end of the Elsecar Branch and hopefully the canal will form part of the industrial story there.[4]

The Dearne & Dove has one more extremity to explore, its southern 'foot'. The canal starts at Swinton, at a junction with the Sheffield & South Yorkshire Navigation. It immediately rises through four locks, the bottom three of which are used as dry-docks by Waddington's boat-yard. Apart from the top lock, very little of the flight is recognisable, but the collection of boats normally in the yard offers an insight into waterways commerce.[5] Above the locks a short stretch is in water, the reason being that this part of the canal was kept open after the rest had closed so that boats could continue to reach Canning Town Glassworks.

IF THE Barnsley Canal and the Dearne & Dove Canal were both restored, they would form a link between the river navigations of Sheffield and Leeds, the creation of a circular route for all canal users—boaters, walk-ers, cyclists, etc. The Barnsley Canal Group is campaigning for such an effort, although the Dearne & Dove's problems with obstructions needs a pragmatic approach, perhaps using the River Dearne to bypass prob-lems in the first miles.

---

4. On the B6097, 'brown-signed' from Junction 36 on the M1.
5. On the A6022 at Swinton, four miles north of Rotherham. Turn into Dun Street by the Red House pub.

The Dearne & Dove at Swinton

Further Reading

Hadfield, Charles, *The Canals of Yorkshire and North East England* (David & Charles). History.

Useful Contacts

Barnsley Canal Group 93 Swinston Hill Road, Dinnington, Sheffield S31 7RY. Tel: 01909 ~~565225.~~ Information available on both canals.

Alan Hall   206498 (01226) (Heart Attack '96)!

Public Transport

Rail Stations (Nearest*) Barnsley, Elsecar, Wombwell, Swinton*.

Places to Visit in the Area

Tourist Information Barnsley. Tel: 01226 206757.
Worsbrough Country Park has an extensive programme of guided walks on various topics. Also wholemeal flour ground in the mill for sale. Wigfield Farm, farm trail, animals, rare breeds. Tel for both: 01226 774527.
Elsecar Heritage Workshops Newcomen engine, steam trains, workshops, bottle museum, crafts. Contact Tourist Information for details.
Cannon Hall Open Farm Cawthorne. Farm animals, donkeys, ponies, wallabies. Tel: 01226 790427.

Alan Hall.,
75 Queens Dri
Barnsley.
S75 2QA.

Monthly meetings in Barnsley,.
4x magazines p.a.

122

The Fossdyke

Navigable; 11 miles long; 1 wide lock
OS map: Landranger sheet 121

OTHER canals may jostle for places in the Industrial Revolution's roll of antiquity honours, but the Fossdyke treats such upstarts with disdain—understandable for a waterway that was sailed by the Danes when they invaded Lincolnshire in AD 870. Built by the Romans to link their colony at Lincoln with the water-highway of the River Trent, the Fossdyke is now the oldest navigable canal in Britain.

At its western end the Fossdyke meets the River Trent at Torksey where a lock links the two waterways; halfway along the eleven-mile course is the small town of Saxilby and the old canal ends in Brayford Pool in the centre of Lincoln. Between those points the Fossdyke is quiet and a typical Lincolnshire waterway where navigation is a bonus from the all-important drainage of the rich fenlands. Nevertheless, for boats it is one section of a strategic waterway system that, together with the River Witham, allows them to cruise from The Wash to the Trent without going round the coast.

TORKSEY is a good spot to indulge in the ever-popular national pastime of boat-watching: a checkpoint between canal and tidal river, a meeting point for a wide variety of craft and easily accessible by road. The lock would not look out of place on the Thames: its colourful garden, hanging baskets, pristine black-and-white paintwork, lock-house and tidy sign-bedecked surroundings are worthy of the upper reaches of the capital's river.[1]

---

1. *Torksey Lock is eight miles south of Gainsborough, clearly signed on the A156, south of Torksey village, with a car park on both sides of the road, toilets, and The Wheelhouse restaurant.*

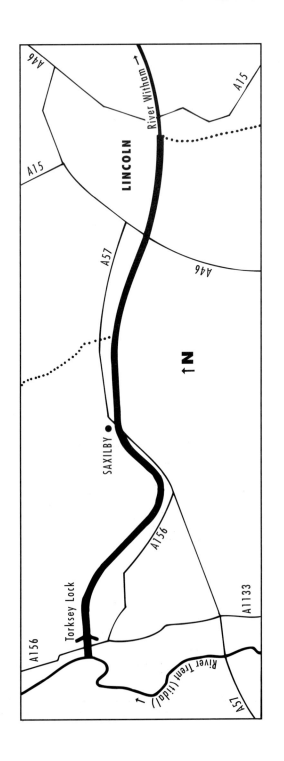

Torksey Lock and moorings

A gate from the car park leads to the area immediately above the lock, an orderly domain where boat crews moor to fill freshwater tanks, empty rubbish bins and toilets, have a shower and generally get their craft and themselves ship-shape. They also check times with the lock-keeper and then wait for the tide on the Trent to turn in the direction they need—ebbing if going downriver to the Chesterfield Canal, the Stainforth & Keadby Canal, or out to the Humber and the North Sea; tide coming in if they are going upriver to Newark, Nottingham and the main canal network. Sometimes there is a slight air of tension among the boat crews. Have we judged the tide right? All the engine checks OK? Everything securely stored away? (It can sometimes be rough on the river when the tide is flowing against the wind.) No stopping until the destination is reached—can the dog last that long without getting off? Have the kids got their life-jackets on? As they go through the lock, the keeper makes a note of where they are going, a radio call to his colleague at the destination lock keeps a check on the whereabouts of boats on the tideway. This is both comforting and disquieting: some-one will be looking out for us, but then again there must be some possi-bility of a mishap or they wouldn't bother to look out! On the other hand, boats coming in from the Trent often exude an air of relief, the quiet confidence of a challenge overcome, a haven reached, a job well done, a sailor home from the sea.

The lock they have passed through has notable features other than the garden; one is the double sets of gates at both ends. Normally, locks are designed to transfer boats between a constant higher level and a constant lower level, but those on a tidal river sometimes have two sets of gates, as at Torksey, to allow operation on the rare occasions when the level of the river is higher than the canal. Another difference at Torksey is that on three sets of gates there is no room for the long balance beams that are normally the most eye-catching feature of locks. Instead there are round, spoked, white-painted windlasses that are turned to open and close the gates. The exceptions are the massive gates by the road bridge, their balance beams towering overhead, but these are only used on exceptionally high tides, perhaps once a year, and moving them takes a great deal of effort by the lock-keeper.

Walking along the water's edge, away from the lock, past the neatly-mown grass banks, the way is barred by a locked white gate that gives security to the boats based at Torksey. However, steps up the bank by the gate give access to the towpath that can be followed for as long as a walker desires. From behind the flood-wall the visitor can look down upon the ranks of moored boats, mostly cruisers but some narrowboats among them. Then further on, alongside a concrete bank, are the visitor moorings for boats passing through, where they can stay for up to three days without charge. This is where any sort of craft may be seen: always pot luck what might be moored—gin-palaces, rust-buckets, commercial tugs, tiny bubbles of cruisers, large coastal craft, yachts—or nothing.

From here the towpath extends into the distance along the top of the grassy floodbank that lines the Fossdyke for most of its course—and allows the walker to look down at the boats that chug past. On the other side of the path the fields head for a distant horizon; birds call and voices drift across on the breeze that often whiffles over the fenlands. Anglers dot the waterline, ducks dabble at the edges and all is peaceful.

However, idyllic as this may be, it's only one of Torksey's two different faces—the other is the tidal River Trent lurking below the lock. Access to the river is across the A156 and through the car park opposite the entrance to the lock area. The lock can be seen under the road bridge, the traffic lights tell approaching boaters if the lock is ready for them: not an easy judgement to make without the lights, from a boat you can see gates but you don't know if they are the bottom gates closed against you or the top ones of an open lock. A grassy bank with a picnic table slopes down to the water but this is not the Trent proper, it's only a side-cut from the river and a refuge where the mooring pontoons change level with the tide.

The Trent itself can be found by walking along the top of the bank, through a white gate and onto the junction with the river. Sometimes the river can look benign and insignificant; other times it seems resentful and confined; if a strong wind is against the flow it can be choppy and fitful. To the right is downstream to the Humber and the North Sea, to the left upstream to the Midlands and the majority of the inland waterways system. If the river's running upstream, the tide's coming in!

From the Trent bank a disparate trio of buildings can be seen. Opposite is the towering enormity of Cottam Power Station, one of the many that use water from the Trent for cooling; downstream, on the near bank, the overawed ruins of Torksey Castle; at the junction a small pumping station that's used by the National Rivers Authority (NRA) to take water from the Trent up into the Fossdyke, from where it's transferred via the Rivers Witham and Ancholme to augment Grimsby's supplies in dry seasons. A stile by the pumping station allows the riverside path to be followed for a number of miles, often a refreshing walk as there's always a cool breeze—or stronger—blowing by the river no matter what the weather is like elsewhere.

FROM TORKSEY the Fossdyke follows an uncomplicated course—long straight stretches in true Roman style for the five miles to Saxilby. The countryside is quiet and the views generous, although boat crews see little of the surroundings as their world is limited by the high grassy floodbanks. The A57 comes alongside for the last mile to Saxilby where it crosses over the waterway on its way to Lincoln, the Fossdyke and the road following much the same route to their shared destination.

Road access to Saxilby is via the B1241, off the A57 bypass. Shops and pubs line the road facing the Fossdyke, their view of the waterway obscured by the ever-present flood defences. A footbridge gives access to the grassy picnic area on the far bank, popular moorings for boats

Saxilby

on sunny summer Sundays when the willows give some shade and the barbecue stands are well used.

Underneath the footbridge can be seen the brick and stone foundations of the swing-bridge that used to carry the road traffic across here before the bypass was built. It was a notorious bottleneck for the old sailing keels that had to wait for the keeper to stop the traffic and wind the bridge out of their way, and the opening was only just wide enough for them to pass through. With only wind power—and that obstructed by the buildings and the banking—it was difficult to manoeuvre the keels, and the crews often had to use the ropes to man-haul the vessels through. A detailed information panel on the abutment shows how the bridge worked; another nearby, tells of Saxilby's Fossdyke history and has a photograph of the old swing-bridge, with the Sun Inn in the background as it still is.

A mile east of Saxilby, the River Till flows into the Fossdyke and the A57 drifts away to leave the waterway in peace. It's a secluded walk along the bank top: distant Lincoln Cathedral and the waterside fishermen are permanent and unmoving features, the birds and boats transient.

The approach to Lincoln along the Fossdyke is lined with moored boats of all sorts. By road the A57 nears the city centre and a right-turn onto Brayford Wharf North gives access to Brayford Pool and a waterside multi-storey car park.

Brayford Pool is an enigma. In other cities a wide expanse of navigable water is a major tourist attraction: buildings jostling for the much-sought-after waterside environment, summer events, prestigious marinas, photogenic boating scenes, etc. Such locations are however a modern leisure focus, and throughout history Lincoln's eyes have looked up the hill to the cathedral and the castle, nowadays surrounded by the cobbled streets and small shops of the tourist brochures. Brayford Pool, as is the nature of water, sits at the foot of the hill and as a result is not part of the city's heart and soul. The Pool has played an important part in Lincoln's trading wealth: in the thirteenth century it was England's fourth largest port; in the eighteenth and nineteenth centuries the wharves were busy with keels bringing grain and seed to the mills, warehouses and breweries that lined the banks. But that was workaday trade. Visitors have always come to see the cathedral, and the many artists who painted Brayford Pool usually chose a scene with the cathedral in the background—today's postcards and photographs of the Pool are no exception.[2]

Having said that, a visit to Lincoln's waterways is a change from the

2. *Over the years many artists have painted Brayford Pool and the rivers in the area; examples of their work can be seen in Lincoln's Usher Art Gallery.*

usual tourist haunts, and a good deal easier on the legs than slogging up the hill. The Fossdyke enters at the western corner where a lift-bridge has to be operated before boats can proceed; a bell is provided to call someone from the nearby works and, reminiscent of another age, the traffic is stopped by a man with a red flag so that the bridge may be raised.

Visiting boats usually call at the moorings by the Harbourmaster's Office. As at Torksey, there are all the services and supplies needed and access is by use of the usual British Waterways' key. Most of the boats based in the Pool are moored on the southern side, but all the banks are lined with something nautical: marinas, boatyards, chandleries, slipways, canoe and cruising clubs. A future plan is for new buildings for the University of Lincoln to stretch along the southern side of the Pool.

Brayford Pool has swans like other places have ducks: they congregate in the north-eastern corner around the River Witham's exit, haughtily watching the many locals and visitors who sit eating, ever vigilant for the contents of sandwich boxes, paper bags, foil wrappings—the elegant necks lowered in unbecoming haste when leftovers tumble their way.

The water exit, near the Royal William pub, is the narrow start of the cruising route to Boston and The Wash but the first highlight for visiting boaters is to go through the Glory Hole—but that's part of the River Witham's story.

Further Reading

Hadfield, Charles, *The Canals of Eastern England* (David & Charles). History.
Robinson, David N., *Lincolnshire Boats and Bridges in Camera* (Quotes Ltd, 1989; ISBN 0-86023-365-0). Old photographs.

Useful Contacts

British Waterways Manager responsible for the canal. Tel: 01636 705584.
Inland Waterways Association Tel: 01469 530138.

Boat Trips

Cathedral City Cruises Brayford Pool, Lincoln. Tel: 01522 546853.
Torksey Leisure Cruises Torksey Lock. Usually booked parties. Tel: 01427 880609.

Boat Hire

Adventure Afloat At Lincoln, hire per day. Tel: 01205 871439.

Angling (See page 206)

First-class fishery, popular with anglers from a wide area. Bream, roach, perch, eels.

Public Transport

Rail Stations (Nearest*) Saxilby*, Lincoln.

Places to Visit in the Area

Tourist Information Lincoln. Tel: 01522 529828/512971
Bransby Home of Rest for Horses Midway between Saxilby and Sturton by Stow. Home of over 100 rescued horses, ponies, donkeys. Open every day. Tel: 01427 788464.
Lincoln The Cathedral and the Castle are open to the public. Various events are held at the Castle throughout the summer. Guided walking tours of the city are available for individuals or groups.
Lincoln Castle Tel: 01522 511068.
National Cycle Museum Brayford Wharf North. Tel: 01522 545091.
The Old Toy Show 26 Westgate. Tel: 01522 520534.
Usher Art Gallery Lindum Road. Tel: 01522 527980.
Museum of Lincolnshire Life Burton Road. Tel: 01522 528448.

The Calder & Hebble Navigation and The Huddersfield Broad Canal

Calder & Hebble Navigation:
Navigable; 22 miles long
27 wide locks; 8 flood-locks/gates

Huddersfield Broad Canal:
Navigable; 4 miles long; 9 wide locks

OS maps: Landranger sheets 104, 110

THE Calder & Hebble Navigation has to be searched for, but when found it has a feature not seen elsewhere—handspikes. Pleasure boats cruise the River Calder in its steep valley, using it to link sections of canal between Wakefield and Sowerby Bridge.

By their very nature, such river navigations are in valley bottoms and as a result often go unseen by road users. The Calder makes sure this is the case: road and rail keep a respectful height on the valley side from a river that is often unruly after heavy rain or snow on the moors. The result of this isolation is that many people drive through the valley totally unaware of the navigation's existence.

Over the centuries the River Calder has been used to carry the trade of Yorkshire's heartland, and over those same centuries a succession of improvements have allowed boats and their cargoes to reach further and further upstream, to Dewsbury, Brighouse and Halifax.

A separate canal, the Huddersfield Broad, was built to link its name town to the navigation. Eventually, the Calder & Hebble, the most westerly of the Humber-linked waterways, became the central part of two

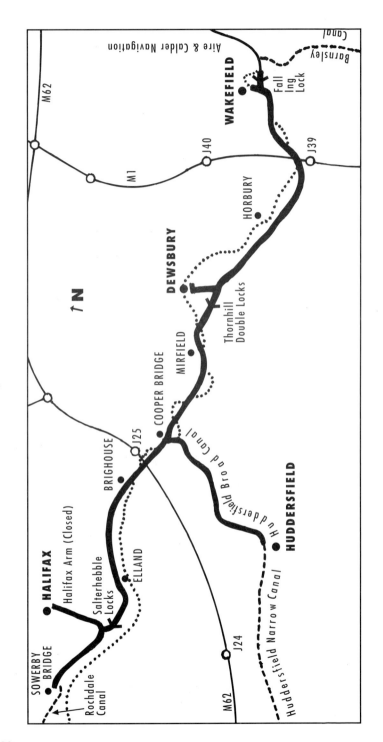

cross-Pennine routes when the Rochdale Canal and the Huddersfield Narrow Canal reached across the hills to bring trade from the west coast. These canals are being restored, and one day the Calder & Hebble will regain its role as the central link in the Yorkshire waterway system.

FOR historical reasons, the Calder & Hebble Navigation begins at Wakefield, seven miles up the River Calder from Castleford.[1] At Fall Ing, boats leave the river and enter the navigation by rising through a lock to a short section of canal that bypasses a weir.

The lock is the great attraction at Fall Ing. On summer Sunday afternoons, ever-changing groups of people watch the boats rise and fall, the crews coming up from the river using ropes to keep their craft under control because the rush of water into this lock can be quite fierce.

At quieter times of the week there is little to see, only in the mind's eye. The basin above the lock was once busy with Tom Pudding compartment

WAKEFIELD

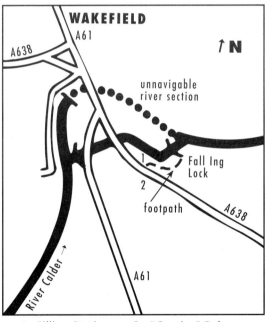

1. Filling Station   2. "Grazier" Pub

---

1. *The mighty Aire & Calder Company made those first seven miles of the river navigable and they are still part of that system. The Calder & Hebble Company was formed in the mid-eighteenth century to extend navigation further upstream from Wakefield to Sowerby Bridge near Halifax.*

133

boats. Their coal cargo came down the chute that's still there in the corner of the basin, although it's now rusted and isolated without coal or boats. When loaded, the Tom Pudding 'trains' were lined up each side of the canal immediately above the lock where they waited for the tugs to take them downriver to Goole. The immense coping stones at the water's edge hint of a substantial past when hobnail boots, hooves and iron-rimmed wheels clattered throughout the day.

Now all is quiet. The rumble of traffic in the background, bird song, noises from nearby workshops, silent moored boats—the normal 'backwater' atmosphere of a city canal. A new walkway promised for 1995 will lead along the waterway from the coal-chute to steps up onto the Doncaster Road bridge, beyond which boats pass through a flood-lock to re-enter the river and there is no towpath.

From here the navigation goes upstream—sometimes river, sometimes canal—and is seldom seen from major roads except where it passes under the M1 where the river is fringed with lakes formed when the earth was extracted for the motorway embankment. The valley floor is still broad and the Calder & Hebble winds its way through nondescript areas, settlements old and new still keeping their distance from the river. The start of a long canal section at Horbury allows buildings to edge the navigation, and the river is some distance from the canal at Dewsbury where a short branch of less than a mile goes to Savile Town Basin and Robinson's boatyard. However, the most charming spot in this area is at the junction, where the branch leaves the main navigation; Thornhill Double Locks are a pleasant background for a picnic and the ever-popular boat-gazing.

Lock Street doesn't look that interesting, but roads with such a name often lead to hidden waterways, sometimes derelict, other times well used as here at Dewsbury. The well-tended locks are worth finding; the secret is to look back where the road crosses the canal branch. Roses grow in front of the little lock-cabin, the grassy banks are well mown, and various trees form a backdrop. In the summer, especially at weekends, a quiet procession of boats passes through the two locks, some stopping to fill their drinking water tanks at the tap alongside. Immediately below the bottom lock is the junction with the Dewsbury branch, where lengthy boats entering or leaving the side-canal need a good deal of manoeuvring to make the tight turn. A picnic on the grass, interspersed with helping boat crews with the gates, has much to recommend it here. The towpath is good in both directions and half a mile downstream is Mill Bank (or Alders) Lock with possibly the oldest chamber in use in Britain, others elsewhere having been completely replaced by centuries of maintenance and improvements.

DEWSBURY–THORNHILL DOUBLE LOCKS

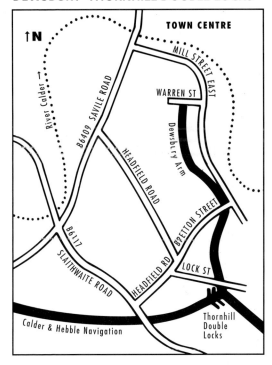

CONTINUING upstream the Navigation passes through Shepley Bridge and Mirfield to the junction with the Huddersfield Broad Canal.[2] This four-mile waterway has nine locks, is still navigable and has a walkable towpath. It's a waterway in waiting—waiting for the completion of the exciting restoration work taking place on its sister canal, the Huddersfield Narrow. When this is finished, Huddersfield's two canals will once again form a boating route across the Pennines. Meanwhile, the Broad Canal waits, like one part of an old double act, ageing in the wings until her partner recovers her health.

But like many an old trooper there is star-quality somewhere, and on the Huddersfield Broad Canal it's a unique lift-bridge. A 'lift-contraption' would be a more descriptive phrase. It has two names—Locomotive Bridge and Turnbridge, neither of which are applicable now, but locomotives used to cross over it, and the previous bridge turned instead of lifting. The easiest way to find it is to walk a short distance along the towpath from Aspley Basin.[3] Ahead will be seen a collection of wheels

2. *Also known as Sir John Ramsden's Canal.*
3. *Aspley Basin is by the A629–B6432 junction in the south-east of Huddersfield city centre.*

and gizmos, dwarfed by a towering mill chimney. At the moment, few boats come along here but you can spend some time working out how the old bridge has operated since 1865. It's all to do with weights, chains, windlasses and muscle.

Turnbridge, or Locomotive Bridge, at Huddersfield

Aspley Basin has a pub and a restaurant, and incessant traffic noise. It's ready for the boats that will come through when the Narrow Canal is restored; until then it's a bit seedy and dead-endish. The most hopeful sight in the basin is the tunnel under the A629: at one time this was blocked off and it took many years of pressure for it to be re-opened. One day boats from Cheshire and Manchester will emerge through it— and then the Turnbridge will be continually up and down like a 100-year-old gymnast.

BACK TO the Calder & Hebble: the waterway continues beyond the junction with the Huddersfield Broad to reach Brighouse where it leaves the Calder for the last time, the river assuming a boatless obscurity as vessels use a canalised section for the rest of the route to Sowerby Bridge. The final six miles have a more intimate, enclosed atmosphere—now that the unpredictable river has been left, the buildings can safely come to the waterside; a towpath allows walkers to share the navigation, and the valley becomes narrower and steep-sided through the ever-higher Pennine hills.

The huddled and elongated towns along this part of the route are also constricted by the valley, almost every building made of the local stone. The textile trade brought wealth and expansion, but now many of the mills and warehouses are empty, monuments to the industrial changes of the last two decades. Those changes have also affected the waterway. Built for trade and now used for leisure, its past and current uses are clearly seen at Brighouse on either side of a bridge—especially on summer Saturdays.

The navigation can be found from the A643 in the centre of Brighouse.[4] From the bridge the towpath is busy with shoppers and pedestrians; on sunny days the many waterside seats are full. On the opposite bank a colourful garden often has a boat moored alongside; by the paved towpath, lampposts are brightly painted to match the seats, and bushes and young trees edge the adjacent areas. On Sundays, in the fishing season, the anglers take over and the bank is dotted with earnest faces, high-tech equipment and tins of maggots. The waterway is not hidden away; it's part of the town and an amenity casually enjoyed by many—not at all what it was intended for.

Echoes of past working days can be felt beyond the next road bridge: a section of canal hardly used by the Saturday shoppers. Here there are no fancy lampposts, no murals, no gardens. Instead there are cobbles, time-worn mills and warehouses, bricked-up doors for cargoes no longer landed, and the stillness of the past. Somehow a sunny day doesn't seem to suit this small part of the Calder & Hebble navigation. It seems to need winter murk to match the surroundings; the gaudy leisure boats look incongruous as they cruise past to the colourful scenes beyond the bridge. What are missing here are the old working boats; the waterway is incomplete without them. Sometimes they come back; one still cruising the north-eastern waterways is *June*, a lovely old craft built for this waterway—she chugs along with mast and sail horizontal until unhindered waters are found. *June* is a rare sight, but *Waylon* can usually be seen at Brighouse, of a much later vintage but a working boat on this navigation nonetheless. She's been converted into a cruising boat by her current owner Colin Richardson—ex-Brighouse lock-keeper—who takes small pre-booked parties on local waterway trips.

The next footbridge is at the entrance to Brighouse basin where two locks start the climb up from the river. This was once the little inland town's transport hub, with boats carrying cargoes from east and west coasts—a safe haven off the river. Now pleasure boats are moored in the loading bays. The lock-keeper's house, by the lower lock, was built with a bow-window so that approaching boats could be seen, and the garden wall is marked with the level reached by a flood in 1866. The two locks are usually centres of activity, the one linking the canal and the river a good opportunity to see handspikes in use.

The Calder & Hebble Navigation is the only waterway on which

4. *There is a large car park opposite the Black Swan, a few yards south of the bridge over the waterway.*

Operating a lock with a handspike

Salterhebble Guillotine Lock

handspikes are still used. They are 3ft 6in lengths of hardwood, just over 2 inches wide at one end, tapering down to a 1.5-inch diameter at the other end. A handspike is put into a ratchet on the lock paddles and worked to and fro to open the sluices. This is an ancient way of operating locks, originally installed because the eighteenth-century boats on this predominantly river navigation used such handspikes to wind their anchor chains in—therefore they could operate the locks with an implement they already had on board.

From Brighouse the waterway continues its climb along the ever-narrowing valley, never far from its parent river; past Elland to the southern edge of Halifax—the town that had originally campaigned for the river to be made navigable up to here. Further down the valley, Wakefield already had river transport for its textiles and Halifax wanted the same advantage as its trade rival. However, while Wakefield is actually on the River Calder, Halifax is not—it's high up on the valley side. So the Calder & Hebble was originally planned to end at Salterhebble, the nearest point to Halifax that could easily be made navigable.

Salterhebble Basin with its three locks is a delight. Little now remains of its trading past; instead it has neatly-mown grassy banks, flower beds, stone walls, and wooded hills as a backdrop.

SALTERHEBBLE LOCKS

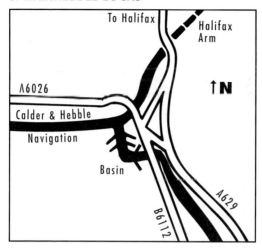

By the top lock is an ivy-clad 'cottage', the affectionate name given to the small buildings erected by the Calder & Hebble Navigation Company along the waterway.[5] A wide area of water links the top two locks, with boat crews carrying handspikes scuttering around it. Both of these locks have normal gates with balance beams, but the third lock, hidden around the bend below the second, is different. Its chamber is near a road bridge and when the road was widened the planners forgot to allow room for the balance beams, so a guillotine gate was installed at the far end. This is power-operated, with the mechanism activated by inserting a BW key. By the guillotine lock are two other Salterhebble features: just before the top gates there is a small aqueduct over the Hebble Brook, and by the bottom gate is a horse-tunnel under the road. As there is no towpath under the bridge, a way was needed, in pre-engine days, for the boat-horses to reach the canal on the other side. They were not massive shires: the whole point of using water transport was that heavy loads could be moved with much less effort than on the muddy roads. The little stone-built tunnel at Salterhebble proves the point and walking through you can almost hear the hooves echoing from the walls.

5. *They can be seen in various states of repair along the Calder & Hebble—Elland Wharf, and Ganny Lock above Brighouse, for example.*

Old warehouses at Sowerby Bridge Basin

The navigation reached Salterhebble in 1767 and the trade of Halifax was brought to it by road; down the steep hills on muddy, rutted roads, many horses struggling to pull incoming raw materials back up to the town. Fifty years of this was enough, and Halifax began to plan a branch canal to bring boats from Salterhebble up to the town. It was a steep climb by road, and it was a steep climb for the boats—in 1.5 miles they rose 100 feet through fourteen locks. Opened in 1828, the bottom section of the Halifax branch is still usable, but none of the locks are, the junction is immediately above the top lock at Salterhebble. At the current end of navigation there's a hotel and a pub: an informative free leaflet—*The Hebble Trail*—is recommended for those who wish to explore further along the Halifax branch on foot.[6]

Although Salterhebble was planned to be the limit of the navigation, it was quickly realised that there would be trade advantages in going a further two miles up the valley to Sowerby Bridge, a small village on an important cross-Pennine road. It didn't remain a small village for long. With a strategic road and a major navigation, the wharf at Sowerby Bridge soon became a busy transhipment point: warehouses, boat-yards, chandlers, and wagon companies flourished. Having reached

6. *Available from Halifax Tourist Information.*

high up into the Pennines, the gentlemen of the Calder & Hebble Navigation Company were well pleased with the trade generated. They were even happier when the Rochdale Canal Company brought its waterway over the hills from the west and the two systems met at Sowerby Bridge. With corn, engineering products, stone, iron, malt, dyestuffs, cotton goods, coal, flax and passengers, the warehouses and wharves were busy.

Today the gritty little West Riding community still has a busy road and needs the bypass planned for 1998. The energetic waterway of the past is now a quiet escape from the present. The mellow yellow stone buildings of the wharf area are still surrounded by clusters of boats, but now they are the hire fleet of Shire Cruisers. The Moorings pub and restaurant is adjacent and Sowerby Marine's chandlery sells nautical bits and bobs. Summer Saturday mornings are busy with hire-boats returning from holidays, the afternoons awash with excited new crews. Overlooking all this, in the background, are the hills that rise in every direction; in the foreground the old buildings echo past boating activities.

The wharf is the very end of the Calder & Hebble Navigation, the end of the 22 miles from Wakefield. However, there is more to see because the Rochdale Canal is just beyond the old warehouses. Only a few yards down the towpath is The Navigation pub and the bridge outside is the route to the other bank and further waterways sights. Across the bridge,

Junction of two waterways at Sowerby Bridge

and back towards the warehouses, an iron post by the towpath marks the start of the Rochdale Canal—past more moored boats to the locks that start that waterway's climb to even higher parts of the valley.

The Rochdale Canal was abandoned in 1952, and after that a stretch in Sowerby Bridge was obliterated when a road was built across it. The removal of that obstruction was the aim of determined local canal enthusiasts and, beyond the locks, is the result of their efforts—a new tunnel opened in 1995 under the offending road, beyond that, a new deep lock. At last Lancashire has been rejoined to one of Yorkshire's most popular waterways—the Calder & Hebble Navigation.

Further Reading

Calder Navigation Society, *West Yorkshire Waterway Guide* (1992; ISBN 09512400-1-3). Available from the Society, see below.

Hadfield, Charles, *The Canals of Yorkshire and North East England* (David & Charles). History.

Smith, Peter L., *Ethel and Angela Jane* (Enterprise Publications, 1976). History of commercial carrying on the Calder & Hebble Navigation.

Useful Contacts

Calder Navigation Society 3 Elm Way, Birstall, Batley WF17 0EQ. Tel: 01924 477571.

British Waterways Manager responsible for the navigation. Tel: 01977 516329.

Boat Trips/Boat Hire

Colin Richardson Brighouse Basin. *MV Waylon*, cruises for up to 12 people. Tel: 01484 713424

Shepley Bridge Marina Tel: 01924 491872. Trips every Sunday and Bank Holidays, narrowboats for hire by the day or longer periods.

Robinsons Dewsbury Basin. *Calder Lady*, large trip-boat for parties. Tel: 01924 467976.

Shire Cruisers Sowerby Bridge. Large fleet of narrowboats for hire. Tel: 01422 832712.

Angling (Main clubs, page 206)

Generally a good quality fishery. Roach, perch, gudgeon, chub, bream.

Public Transport

Rail Stations (Nearest*) Sowerby Bridge, Huddersfield, Mirfield*,
   Wakefield-Westgate.

Places to Visit in the Area

Tourist Information Halifax. Tel: 01422 368725.
Eureka! Halifax. Award winning hands-on museum for children up to age 12.
   Tel: 01426 983191.
Walkley Clogs Hebden Bridge. Britain's only clog manufacturers
   Tel: 01422 842061.
The Calderdale Way 50-mile circular walking route, leaflet from Halifax
   Tourist Information.

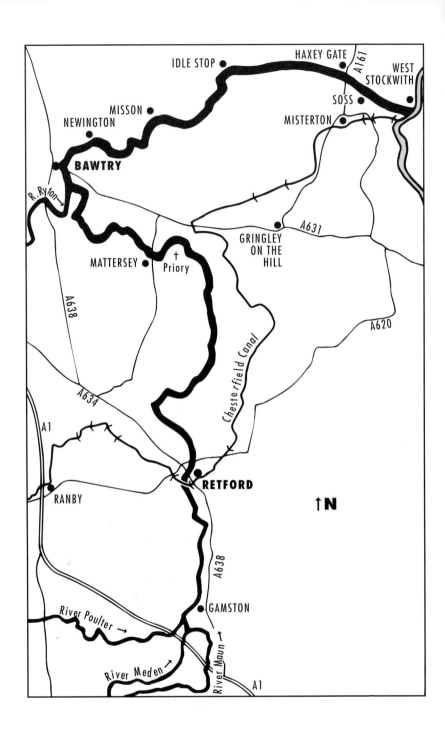

The River Idle

Navigable to Bawtry; 26 miles long
No locks or tunnels
OS map: Landranger sheets 120, 111, 112

CONFINED between floodbanks, obediently flowing when and where ordered, and generally boatless, the Idle has nothing of a liberated river's generous nature. But if fresh air and exercise are required, the paths along the tops of the grassy floodbanks give walkers access to mind-clearing wide open spaces—far from roads and railways, with manicured fields spreading to a distant encircling horizon. Bawtry's Sunday market is popular, as is Retford's market square on Thursdays and Saturdays. Mattersey has a riverside thirteenth-century priory, and Misson and West Stockwith are villages of quiet charm.

The Idle is a reclusive river; its only uncharacteristic foray into the limelight a graceful passage through King's Park in the centre of Retford. However, in its earlier forms the Idle is anything but unnoticed—it is created by the merging of the rivers Poulter, Meden and Maun and consists of water that has flowed through the grounds, and formed the lakes, of Nottinghamshire's much-visited Clumber Park, Welbeck Abbey, Thoresby Hall, and Rufford Abbey.

Such illustrious surroundings are lost when the Idle is formed. The previously aristocratic water flows north through quiet countryside before turning eastwards at Bawtry, finally at West Stockwith becoming the last substantial tributary of the River Trent.

But it was not always so—the Idle is a river of past glories. For 500 years boats came ten miles upriver from the Trent to Bawtry, which was throughout that time a substantial inland port. However the nearby Chesterfield Canal and the railways ruined Bawtry's trade and there is little evidence of it today.

The Idle's other major role was, and still is, the control of water in the lowlands near the Trent. Natural marshlands, the area was drained in the early 1600s by the Dutch engineer Vermuyden. Since then the river has been the central component of a vast network of channels that protect what is now valuable agricultural land. In addition, the tides of the Trent are kept out of the Idle by gates and a pumping station at West Stockwith. Passage through these barriers by boats is being discussed, but the fees proposed by the NRA are high and as a result the chances of a visitor seeing a boat on the Idle are remote.

Open countryside, fresh air and bird song are however in plentiful supply.

Retford

IT IS SAID that Retford owes the original version of its name to the River Idle—hooves and feet churned the clay banks of a ford and turned the water red, hence 'Redford'. This unlocated ford may have named the town, but it did no harm to river users; the same cannot be said of another of Retford's Idle crossings, this time in King's Park. Here the Chesterfield Canal is carried across the river on a muscular aqueduct built in 1774—three years later competition from the completed canal

146

took most of the trade from Bawtry's port and the Idle's boats, never to return.

Within King's Park the river bubbles over gentle weirs, the rolling grassland of one bank linked to the flowerbeds on the other by well-used footbridges. Paths follow the river through the town, but there is little to recommend it: the border between the boroughs of West and East Retford, the Idle is still left in a void between the two.

Flowing north the river leaves the gentle hills of the Retford area and heads towards the flat landscape of the Trent valley. Public footpaths along the banks are infrequent here and the Idle can mostly be seen from nearby roads as it twists and turns through variously cropped farmlands.

Mattersey Priory

The remains of Mattersey Priory—and 'remains' is a good word for the site—is managed by English Heritage. Founded in 1185, the brothers of the Order of St Gilbert of Sempringham lived by the River Idle in what became, over the centuries, a large establishment. Signposted from Mattersey village, the priory is quite a distance down a potholed track, the river usually unseen beyond the fenced enclosure with its information panel.

Having been joined by the Ryton, the volume of water in the Idle is noticeably greater by the time Bawtry is reached. In wet winters this extra flow is allowed to flood the meadows alongside the railway viaduct, forming great shallow lakes. From here to the Trent, the Idle's drainage function is paramount and the river's behaviour is tightly controlled by the NRA at the pumping station downstream at Stockwith.

Even though Bawtry's road borders are proudly signed '12th Century

Port', it has to be admitted that little evidence remains of that busy era, even though it lasted until the late 1700s. There is a Wharf Street and some nearby houses that could have been owned by merchants, but the only obvious pointer to a trading port is a pub called 'The Ship', on the A631 to Gainsborough. Basic descriptions of the boats that traded on the Idle have survived but, try as it might, the little river never managed to carry a vessel as shown on the pub's sign—a three-masted

The incongruous pub sign at Bawtry

merchantman, sails billowing on the open sea, and flying a Union Jack (illegal on such a vessel since 1634!).

The reason for the paltry lack of port artifacts is that as one transport system lapsed, another took its place. Between 1780 and 1830 Bawtry took advantage of its position on the old Great North Road and the prosperity of the coaching era. The town was almost completely rebuilt at that time, and turned its back on the old river. Then the railways arrived, with the building of what is now the east-coast mainline between London and Scotland. The tracks are carried above the riverside meadows on a many-arched viaduct, cutting the Idle off from the town wharves where so much trade used to take place. However the old course of the river can be seen on an Ordnance Survey map because here the waterway is the Nottinghamshire–Yorkshire border, which follows the old course of the Idle, not where it flows now.

At Newington another Ship Inn hides behind a floodbank, its sign showing an even taller-masted vessel, but at least it has no illegal flags.

Misson's pub associated with the Idle was the Ferry Boat Inn, but that closed some years ago; the actual ferry disappeared even earlier. It used to operate from the end of River Lane, a quiet road that slopes down to the Idle from near the village's fifteenth-century church. This is the start of the easily-accessible section of the river and a peaceful footpath leads downstream on the ever-present grassy floodbank. Bird songs drift across the fields and the solitude is wonderful. Alongside, the Idle dutifully flows where bidden, its days of exploring the surrounding lowlands many centuries in the past. Heavy prolonged rainfall still does however, give the river expansionist ideas and one of its escape routes is evident a little distance from Misson. Set into the floodbank is a concrete slope over which the Idle can escape into a relief channel when water levels exceed a set height—the footpath is carried across on an upper level.

Two miles downstream from Misson is Idle Stop, the accurately-named point where the seventeenth-century Dutch engineers stopped the river from flowing further north along its natural course to the River Don. Instead they turned it eastwards to the Trent along a man-made waterway that was even then ancient—the Bycarsdyke. Thus diverted, the Idle's course becomes straighter, eventually reaching the Gate Inn at Haxey Gate, one mile north of Misterton. The A161 crosses on a modern structure, but alongside is its predecessor: a lovely single-span stone bridge by the pub. The Gate Inn has a children's play area, dovecotes and ponies and from across the road the riverbank can be walked for the final two miles to the Trent.

However, the easiest way to see the features along the last stretch of the Idle is to drive to West Stockwith. The village straggles along the Trent, the buildings peeking over the flood defences at the roofs of East Stockwith on the far bank. There used to be a ferry between the twin villages, but that finished many years ago, it is now eleven miles by road, via the bridge at Gainsborough. The Idle flows under the road and into the Trent, with a car park at the junction of the two waterways. From here the Idle can be walked on both banks, although the southern (left) side is the most popular.

Only a few yards upriver is a powerful guillotine gate. At West Stockwith the Trent is tidal, its level therefore constantly variable. At high tide, and allowing for the amount of freshwater coming down both rivers, the level in the Trent for a number of hours can be higher than that in the Idle. On such occasions the gate is lowered to keep the Trent out of the smaller river. This defence was installed in 1938 but it did not solve all the problems and flooding still occurred in the Idle valley.

Four hundred yards further upstream is the answer to those problems—a £2 million pumping station built in 1978. Here the Idle can be kept flowing—and therefore draining the land—no matter what levels are in the Trent. Powerful pumps can discharge the Idle's water by raising it to the higher Trent whenever necessary. The operations here and at the guillotine gate are automatic, controlled by sensors in the Trent at Owston Ferry which detect the direction of the flow and water level.

Misterton Soss

Two flood defences have been seen, from 1938 and 1978, but predating them both is Misterton Soss. A little further upriver the twin brick chimneys of the Soss still tower over the Idle, the first built in 1828, the second in 1838. Between the two buildings is a channel called the Mother Drain: now valued and protected for its plants and insect life, it once played a vital role in keeping the area dry. The famous engineer William Jessop devised a plan whereby all the other ditches in the lowlands on this bank of the Idle discharged their waters into the Mother Drain. This in turn was pumped up into the Idle by a 40hp steam engine installed in Misterton Soss. The second engine-house was built ten years later to help with the volumes involved. The entrances to the old buildings are now boarded up for safety reasons, but the lofty windows and high chambers are potent reminders of the ponderous power of the beam engines that worked here for 100 years—keeping 4,000 acres of fertile farmland drained. One building still has a set of old wooden gates in place in the Mother Drain, angled to allow the water to flow in only one direction.

150

An unusual circular walk is possible from the Soss—a signed path goes one mile to Misterton and the towpath of the Chesterfield Canal at the Packet Inn. Turning left along the towpath, the canal can be followed to its junction with the Trent at Stockwith Basin.[1] From here a left turn can be made along the road back to the Idle and the car park at West Stockwith, or a third waterway can be walked by using the Trent's floodbank to the same destination.

This circular walk is informative because it was the canal that ruined the trade on the Idle—and brought the prosperous days of West Stockwith village to an end. For centuries the busy shipping traffic on the Trent used to call at Stockwith's wharves. Cargoes were stored and transhipped between vessels on the two rivers, boats were built and repaired, and merchants prospered and lived in houses worthy of their status. Times were good, but it all ended with the coming of the canal. Trade went to the more reliable new waterway, and the Idle's boats and Stockwith's wharves were no longer required. Little evidence remains of the prosperous days, but the village has buildings of a wide variety of styles, sizes and ages strung out along its one road. The church by the car park has the date 1722 over the door, and a cottage further along has 1741 marked on the wall. Next door is Ropery House, the remaining section of the extensive works where miles of ships' rigging was made. The three-storeyed houses by the Trent are those built for the wealthy merchants; one such is Stradbroke House with its walled garden.

West Stockwith ends abruptly; walking back on the Trent floodbank gives a different view of the houses already observed, and the possibility of seeing one of the sea-going vessels that go up to Gainsborough when the tide is right.

The River Idle is a waterway of past glories. Its current role may appear mundane in comparison, but the river is nevertheless vital to the area through which it flows, undertaking a crucial drainage service of which few people are aware—not spectacular, but steady. The one thing the river has never been is idle.

1. Stockwith Basin is included in the chapter on the Chesterfield Canal, page 153.

Further Reading

Davy, Sam, *Nottinghamshire Rivers* (Ashbracken, 1991; ISBN 1-872356-05-2).
Hadfield, Charles, *The Canals of the East Midlands* (David & Charles). History.

Useful Contacts

Inland Waterways Association Tel: 01302 873127.

Public Transport

Rail Station Retford.

Places to Visit in the Area

Tourist Information Retford. Tel: 01777 860780.
Miniature World Museum of toys. West Stockwith, opposite car park, next to
    White Hart. Tel: 01427 890982.

The Chesterfield Canal

46 miles long; 31 miles navigable, the remainder in various states of restoration

6 wide locks, 59 narrow locks, 2 tunnels

OS map: Landranger sheets 119, 120, 111, 112

The current state of the restoration work can be obtained by contacting the Chesterfield Canal Society.

THE Chesterfield Canal is a charming channel of solitude: a little waterway that starts at the edge of Derbyshire's Peak District, passes through Yorkshire hills, and then picks its way across rural Nottinghamshire to the River Trent. The towpath is popular as a long distance walk called the Cuckoo Way, its waters are a haven for wildlife, the engineering features are treasured by historians, and the overall atmosphere is enjoyed by boaters, artists, photographers and anglers.

The canal looks as if it's been there forever, but like all the other waterways in this book, the Chesterfield was developed for commercial reasons: to carry cargoes and earn money. It is a quiet, delightful remnant of another age. The inconspicuous little canal was once the glory of the area, built by James Brindley, one of Britain's most famous engineers. It was a new transport system for the young Industrial Revolution—one of the earliest products of the first Canal Age in the 1770s.

Today the Chesterfield is regaining its fame as a wonderful example of the canal age, but this time it's because of the restoration schemes that are rescuing the abandoned sections at the western end. The achievements of the 1770s were great flights of staircase locks and one of England's longest canal tunnels—now they are the challenge of the 1990s.

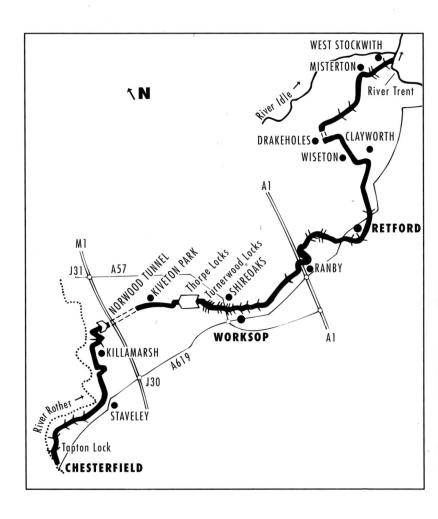

THE FAMOUS crooked spire has seen it all. In 1777 Chesterfield's parish church looked down at the navvies celebrating the completion of the town's new canal. In the 1990s it has watched over the volunteers of the Chesterfield Canal Society as they have laboured to return the old waterway to its past glory. The results of this recent effort can be seen at Tapton Lock, now fully restored together with substantial lengths of canal and towpath. An easy way to see what has been achieved is to take a trip here on the Society's boat *John Varley*, named after Brindley's assistant engineer who was responsible for most of the original construction work.[1]

A newly restored section, overlooked by Chesterfield's famous crooked spire

Above Tapton Lock the popular tree-fringed towpath follows the restored canal to Tapton Mill Bridge. This is a pretty little structure with curving brickwork that clearly shows that this end of the Chesterfield is a narrow canal, for boats less than seven feet wide. Common in the Midlands, it is nevertheless rare in this area where the waterways are dominated by river-based navigations; indeed the Chesterfield is the only waterway in this book with this type of lock. Further along its route, the little canal has other features not found elsewhere in this area.

Beyond the bridge the canal merges into the River Rother for another few hundred yards, the towpath continuing to the limit of navigation alongside Holbeck Close, not far from the railway station.

1. *Off the A61/A619 (Tesco) roundabout, on the northern edge of Chesterfield; 'brown-signed' to the canal. Contact the Canal Society for details of the trip-boat and the promotional 'canal day' events.*

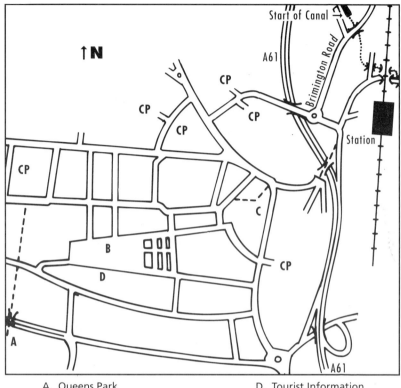

A. Queens Park
B. Market Square
C. "Crooked Spire"
D. Tourist Information
CP. Car Park

BELOW Tapton Lock the canal starts its journey to the Trent, following the valley of the River Rother to Brimington and Staveley. Because the restoration is ongoing, it is not possible to say at the time of writing which areas have been completed, but the first five miles should be done by 1996, including a further four locks.

Eventually the canal has to leave the Rother's valley to make its way eastward—but there is a ridge of Yorkshire hills in the way. The turn is made near Killamarsh and the waterway soars up the flanks of the hills with thirteen locks in one-third of a mile, the great Norwood flight.[2] This will probably be the last section to be restored, so the locks will remain derelict and overgrown for some time. In the winter when the vegetation dies down, the four sets of staircase chambers can be seen, and the side-ponds that supplied them with water. The building by the bottom

2. *The canal is signed on the A618 north of Killamarsh, near the Angel Inn.*

*Quiet countryside
near Hayton*

Shireoaks

Drakeholes Tunnel

lock was once the Boatman Inn, more recently a private residence, it was badly damaged by fire in 1994. The house halfway up the flight is a converted water-powered sawmill. The towpath here is a public right of way, but it is on private property so please respect the owner's privacy.

Just beyond the top lock, and a struggle in summer along the overgrown towpath, can be found the reason for the restoration work being delayed on the locks—the sealed western portal of Norwood Tunnel. One and three-quarter miles through the hillside (2,893 yards), this was the longest canal tunnel in Britain when it was completed in 1775, and it still rates high in the all-time list. It is completely straight and passes through the hill and under the M1 where the motorway runs along the top of the ridge. Plans are in hand for an easily-walkable path to be made over the tunnel. If you wish to see the tunnel, it is much easier to find the eastern portal, an easy walk from Kiveton Park station with the towpath on the far bank from the railway.

The local council has published plans for the canal at Kiveton Park— restoration, visitors' centre, boat-trips—so things may change here. One subject they are sure to highlight is that the stone used to build the Houses of Parliament was quarried nearby, in the pre-railway 1830s, and brought to a wharf near the level crossing. Here it was loaded into narrowboats and taken along the canal to West Stockwith, where it was transhipped into Trent sloops for the journey round the coast and up the Thames to Westminster.

The most popular walking area on the canal is eastwards from Kiveton Park; along the summit pound, winding through wooded quiet areas, keeping level by hugging the contours of the hillside in true Brindley style. Then down the eastern flank of the hills via the fifteen locks of the Thorpe/Turnerwood flight. Fortunately, this stretch has always remained water-filled because it carries the supply for the navigable sections of the canal in Nottinghamshire. As a result, the wildlife and plants here have thrived and the canal is a quiet haven for all visitors. Halfway down the locks, the hamlet of Turnerwood is a favourite with photographers and artists. Continuing down the hills the canal reaches Shireoaks where a nearby station offers towpath walkers return transport to Kiveton Park.[3]

Where the navigable section of the canal starts depends on the restoration progress, but at the time of writing it was at Worksop. Boats have always been able to use the remaining 26 miles to the River Trent, the efforts of local enthusiasts in the 1960s having saved them from

3. *This train service may be restricted on Sundays. Canal restoration schemes now in progress may temporarily hinder access between Kiveton Park and Worksop. Latest details from British Waterways, page 160.*

abandonment. Leaving Worksop, the little canal wanders out into the relatively flat Nottinghamshire countryside to Retford, offering only solitude and peace. Numerous quiet country roads give access to various points—the tunnel and pub at Drakeholes, the boats moored at Clayworth, and the estate village of Wiseton. It's a world apart from ambitious restoration schemes, great lock flights and a blocked tunnel under the M1—but it is the same waterway.[4]

The canal-side Packet Inn at Misterton[5] is half a mile from the end of the waterway, a wide and straight towpath linking the pub to West Stockwith Basin and the tidal and unpredictable Trent. In the past the basin was where cargoes were transhipped between canal and river craft, although the narrowboats did regularly venture out onto the river even though they were not designed for such a waterway. Now the basin is a haven for leisure use, with safe moorings off the river for a varied collection of vessels: narrowboats, cruisers, coastal craft and yachts.

The activity at the great lock down from the basin to the Trent depends on the state of the tide; a minimum depth of water in the river is needed before boats can pass in and out of the chamber. Also crews will wait for the flow to take them in the direction they wish to travel; much consultation of tide tables is needed when planning a departure. Different problems face river arrivals who sometimes have a difficult task in crossing the current to enter the lock, especially the narrowboats with their flat-bottomed hulls. If you see one having problems getting into the lock from the river, make allowances in your judgement, for it is a tricky, and sometimes tense manoeuvre.

Sometime in the future, boats—at least those narrow enough—will once again be able to cruise from this river-dominated scene up into the heart of Derbyshire. The old crooked spire is waiting. It hasn't seen a boat from the Trent since 1907; the canal enthusiasts in its shadow are determined that it will not wait too much longer. In the meantime you can already enjoy the quiet charms of an historic and rural waterway—the Chesterfield Canal.

---

4. The Norwood Packet *trip-boat is operated in the Retford/Clayworth area by the Chesterfield Canal Society.*

5. *North-west of Gainsborough, just off the A161 where it crosses the canal in Misterton.*

Further Reading

Richardson, Christine, and John Lower, *A Walkers' and Boaters' Guide to the Chesterfield Canal and Cuckoo Way* (Sheffield: The Hallamshire Press, 1994; ISBN 1-874718-25-3). Price: £5.95.

Richardson, Christine, *The Waterways Revolution: From the Peaks to the Trent* (1992; ISBN 1-85421-161-7). The construction of the Chesterfield Canal, 1768–1778.

Hadfield, Charles, *The Canals of the East Midlands* (David & Charles). History.

Useful Contacts

Chesterfield Canal Society The Secretary, 18 Rosedale Avenue, Chesterfield S40 2UY. Tel: 01246 559054.

British Waterways Manager responsible for the canal. Tel: 01636 705584.

Inland Waterways Association Tel: 01302 873127.

Boat Trips

Operated by the Chesterfield Canal Society.

The Norwood Packet Retford/Clayworth area. Tel: 01246 812313.

The John Varley Chesterfield area. Tel: 01246 274077.

Angling (Main clubs, page 206)

Heavily stocked with chub, roach, perch, bream, carp. The thick weed growth in some areas and the clear water often make fishing difficult.

Public Transport

Rail Stations (Nearest*) Chesterfield, Kiveton Park*, Shireoaks*, Worksop, Retford.

Places to Visit in the Area

Tourist Information Chesterfield. Tel: 01246 207777
Retford. Tel: 01777 860780
Worksop. Tel: 01909 501148

Chesterfield Summer markets, street entertainers. The 'crooked spire' of St Mary and All Saints is open to the public most Bank Holidays and some other days. Tel: 01246 206506.

Rother Valley Country Park Near Killamarsh. 300-hectare park, footpaths and cycle routes, old mill, large lakes for watersports and angling. Tel: 0114 247 1452.

Clumber Park Near Worksop. 3,800 acres of parkland with 80-acre lake, cycle hire, restaurant, shop. National Trust. Tel: 01909 476592.

The Mayflower Trail A road tour around the peaceful Nottinghamshire villages with Pilgrim Fathers connections. Leaflet from Retford Tourist Information.

Peak District National Park 524 square miles, 5,000 miles of public footpaths.

Chatsworth House Home of the Duke and Duchess of Devonshire. Farmyard and adventure playground, farm shops, lakes, 100-acre garden, 1,000 acres of landscaped parkland. Tel: 01246 582204.

Castleton. Underground boat trips in Speedwell Cavern. Tel: 01433 620512. Also Blue John Cavern. Tel: 01433 620638.

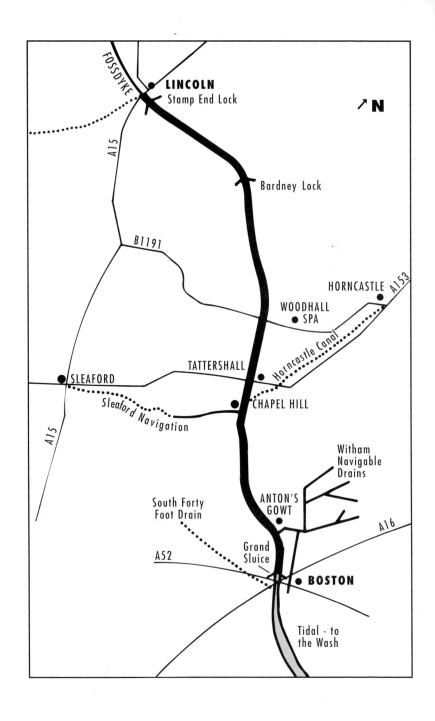

The River Witham

70 miles long, 36 miles navigable; 3 wide locks
OS map: Landranger sheets 121, 122, 131

THE Witham is a river of two halves. From Grantham it is a natural and unnavigable waterway flowing north to Lincoln; at Lincoln it meets the Fossdyke and turns to the east through a strategic gap in the hills, and changes completely to become the second link in the boaters' route to Boston and The Wash.

Centuries of transport and drainage improvements have resulted in the navigable Witham retaining hardly any natural features. It has been chopped and channelled by numerous engineers and continues to be a major part of Lincolnshire's water management system—but it's still a waterway of variety.

This book concentrates on the river from Lincoln to Boston, where past and present activities provide much of interest—including one of England's most famous bridges.

THE River Witham flows quietly into the south-eastern corner of Lincoln's Brayford Pool, little noticed as it goes under the railway and past a slipway usually covered in preening swans. Few visitors find this corner of the Pool; local people use the footpath as a short cut, fishermen sit immobile, and narrowboat owners go to their craft that are moored nearby. The Witham's arrival in the Pool is unobtrusive—but the river's exit, judging by the accents and languages heard, must feature in tourist photographs carried to homes all over the world.

Within a few yards of its quiet arrival point, the Witham enters the spotlight of 'tourist' Lincoln and, overlooked by the city's magnificent cathedral, flows out of the Pool at Brayford Head: a busy area where boat-trips start, customers sit outside the waterside Royal William pub, office and shop workers eat their sandwiches, and the ever-present swans watch for offered food.

From this narrow outlet the river passes between high-sided buildings, squeezed towards one of the most famous features on England's waterways—the unique and splendid High Bridge, also known as the Glory Hole.

From Brayford Head there's a footpath on both sides of the Witham, but I think it best to take the one on the opposite bank to the cathedral, accessible from the road that crosses the river. This path is less busy and gives a better view of the ancient bridge.

The ancient High Bridge, or Glory Hole

The Glory Hole is the oldest bridge in this country that still has buildings upon it. The span over the Witham is Norman, and underneath, although difficult to see other than from a boat, it is vaulted from points along the centre of the river. The bridge had shops on it in the fourteenth-century, but improvements were made in the 1540s, including the erection of the beautiful half-timbered Tudor buildings that make the Glory

Hole such an unforgettable sight. Narrow staircases at the side take the footpaths up to the busy, but traffic-free, High Street that crosses the river on the bridge; from the quiet of the Witham to the bustle of a busy city. The footpaths continue along the river from across the High Street and now the Glory Hole can be seen from the other side.

Lincoln, with the High Bridge (Glory Hole) in the background

For all its antiquity and beauty, the bridge was a terrible bottleneck for the working boats that brought prosperity to Lincoln. In the 1790s the water under the bridge was too shallow for heavily-laden boats; they were unloaded one side, the cargo carried across the High Street, and reloaded the other side. The porters made a fortune, but all the other traders wanted a solution found. There was a plan to replace the bridge with another but, thankfully, it was rejected as too expensive. Instead engineer William Jessop solved the problem by lowering the river bed and rearranging the water levels to compensate, thereby allowing loaded boats to pass under the reprieved Glory Hole.

The Witham continues through a pleasant area, where Lincoln shows what can be achieved if a waterway is made part of the busy life of a city, rather than hidden away as an anachronism. Modern traffic-free shopping districts stretch along both river banks, linked by footbridges and liberally supplied with waterside seats. Old pubs such as The Witch and the Wardrobe have been incorporated into the scheme and add to the Witham's fine passage through Lincoln.

However, Lincoln is not only a tourist city; it also has an industrial face, although less so than in the past. Signs of that past are further along the river, beyond the A15, where the banks are lined with nineteenth-century mills such as Doughty's, where pure linseed cake for cattle feed used to be produced. Engineering works also stretch for some distance as the river widens and arrives at Stamp End Lock with its weir alongside.

This weir controls the water level of the Fossdyke and the upstream Witham, and it is where Jessop altered the depth when his scheme saved the Glory Hole. Boats avoid the weir by passing through the adjacent Stamp End Lock, its single top gate a guillotine type that goes up and down instead of swinging. This type of gate is very simple, although it must be operated slowly if there is a boat in the lock, as it allows a tremendous force of water through as it rises. The gate is power-operated by boat crews and activated by the usual BW key; the control panel has clearly-labelled instructions, and until the whole process of opening and closing the gate is complete it will not allow the removal of the key.

The Witham is a river, but its flow and behaviour are strictly controlled and it now leaves the city for the flat Lincolnshire fenlands where all water systems are used for drainage and/or storage, depending on the season and the rainfall. That is why British Waterways has installed floating pontoon moorings along the river: if the levels have to be altered overnight then a boat will come to no harm. Further downstream the Witham even has an annual 'closed season' for the same reasons. From 1st November to 1st April the following year mooring is prohibited between Chapel Hill and Boston, a National Rivers Authority ruling so that boats do not complicate the winter water controls. During that period the NRA lowers the river two feet at Boston to create extra capacity for winter rain and snow.

Straightened between confining banks, the Witham makes its way to Bardney Lock where it turns to the south-east and out into the fenlands. The glory, excitement and tourist photographs of Lincoln are now a world away as the river takes on its vital role as the central part of the intricate web of waterways that keep over a quarter of a million acres of this low-lying area drained. On both sides ditches of various sizes make their way to the Witham, peeking through the river's banks and stretching into the distance through rich arable farmlands. In other areas enthusiasts rumble on about what various waterways should be called— canal, river, navigation? In the fenlands of eastern England they scorn such prosaic terms; instead they have a thesaurus of waterways—Hammond Beck, Skerith Drain, Clay Dike, Gill Syke, Timberland Delph, Billinghay Skirth, Barlings Eau.

Few roads approach the Witham and traffic has only four bridges across the river between Lincoln and Boston. Footpaths and the embankments of dismantled railways edge the river, the grassy banks often dotted with anglers because the Witham is one of the great fishing waters; clubs and associations come from a wide area to take part in serious matches.

Kirkstead Bridge crosses to nearby Woodhall Spa—a small town with a distinctive Edwardian air, typical of the many places that became prosperous as visitors 'took the waters'. There's a shop selling all kinds of flying memorabilia, and in a garden a dam-shaped monument to the Dambusters of World War II: the first indications of the area's close association with the RAF, past and present. A little further downriver Coningsby is an active RAF airfield and midweek quiet is often shattered by low flying jets, although for an aircraft enthusiast, cruising the Witham here is a mixture of two delights. Others less enamoured by noise can avoid it because, unless there's a national emergency, the RAF doesn't fly at weekends—but it's always worth keeping an eye on the sky because Coningsby is also the home of the Battle of Britain Memorial Flight. Spitfires, Hurricanes and a Lancaster bomber still fly over the Witham on their way to and from various displays, their hangar the one part of RAF Coningsby that's open to the public.

Neighbouring Tattershall has an extensive water-leisure park, and an impressive castle from the top of which can be seen the nearby Horncastle Canal, making its way to the river at Dogdyke. A short distance downstream, on the opposite bank, the Horncastle's sister waterway, the Sleaford Navigation, meets the Witham at Chapel Hill. Both built in the 1790s the two canals link their name towns to the Witham, thereby gaining access to trade outlets in Boston and the rest of the waterway system via the Fossdyke and the Trent.

The Witham covers the remaining ten miles to Boston in three no-nonsense straight, secluded stretches; roads only come near at Langrick Bridge and by the lock at Anton's Gowt, the entrance to the Navigable Drains. This is a vast network of fenlands waterways that are used to supply water for irrigation in dry seasons and for drainage of the land in wet weather. When they were built it was soon realised that they also provided a means of transport and boats of a suitable size can still cruise many of them. They are an acquired taste, but if you want to go boating on a summer Bank Holiday without seeing another vessel, then go down the Drains. Outside the fishing season people will be few and far between!

WITHAM NAVIGABLE DRAINS

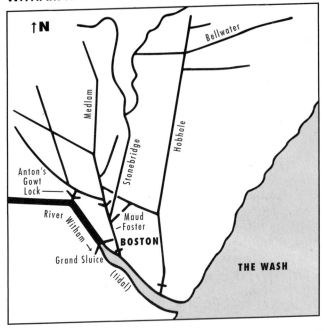

The approach to Boston, by road or river, is reminiscent of childhood outings to the seaside—but instead of competing to see who can see the sea first, it's who can see Boston Stump first. St Botolph's is the riverside parish church and its distinctive tower can be seen for many miles across the flat landscape, its lack of a spire resulting in its affectionate 'Stump' nickname.

At Boston, as it did at Lincoln, the Witham undergoes another of its transformations—from a controlled inland waterway carrying mainly pleasure craft to a tidal river with commercial docks and sea-going ships. The divide between the two is the Grand Sluice, the barrier that holds back much of the river and sets the level between here and Bardney Lock, and stops the tidal waters from The Wash from spreading inland. The great majority of pleasure craft stay on the controlled side of the Sluice, some cruising back upriver, others stopping to visit the town and tying up at the moorings that line the bank. However, vessels wishing to reach the coast can pass through the lock and enter the Witham's last six, tidal, miles, after having reported to the lock-keeper whose office is close by. On rare occasions narrowboats do go through the lock, using The Wash to gain access to the rivers Nene or Great Ouse, but as they are not suited to coastal cruising they have to be very careful about weather and tide conditions, and usually go in company with

Sibsey Trader Windmill, by one of the Navigable Drains

Waiting for the tide at Boston, overlooked by the town's famous 'Stump'

other craft. The Wash is notorious for its moving sandbanks and the narrow channels through them; charts updated with the very latest information are necessary and many skippers who don't know the waters take a local man as a pilot.

It is worth taking a look at the river on the downstream side of the Grand Sluice; depending on the state of the tide, and the controls on the Witham, you will see either a wide navigable waterway or a muddy gutter with a small trickle through the middle of it. On my first visit all I saw was a sea of mud through Boston, only the knowledge that boats could use the river convincing me that it could look different. By contrast, a later visit was at the top of a spring tide—the water was so high a cruiser coming in from the sea had to wait for the level to subside before it could pass under Town Bridge to reach the Grand Sluice!

Overlooking all this activity, as it has for centuries, is the tower of St Botolph's, the largest parish church in England and the great glory of Boston. If you feel fit enough to climb the hundreds of steps to the top of the Stump you will be rewarded with unforgettable views of the Witham, the flat magnificence of the fens, the coast—and bustling Boston down below, its interesting shops and markets, and often-forgotten docks.

Boston's position on a navigable inlet of The Wash has always been the basis of its prosperity, especially the wool trade in the fourteenth century. Today commercial vessels still make their way up the Witham, but not into the town centre because of the river's narrowness and the bridges; the fishing fleet moors alongside London Road, and the large ships enter the busy docks further downriver, or unload at a quay along-side. Aspects of Boston's maritime past and present can be seen by following the road along the west bank of the river: the Ship Inn, Boston Boats chandlery, perhaps the moored mussel fleet and, on the site of the Crown & Anchor, a plaque to George Bass who discovered Bass Straight and played a large part in the history of Australia and Tasmania.

The river bends away from the road where it is joined by the South Forty Foot Drain, yet another major waterway discharging into the Witham. A footpath continues along the bank and the docks can be seen across the river, the entrance lock only operable at certain states of the tide. Containers are stacked up, fork-lift trucks and lorries dart about, cranes tower above; and ships can be seen from various countries, often Germany and Norway.

Looking across at such activity, it's difficult to believe that the river that makes it possible is the same one that timidly enters Brayford Pool, proudly flows through the Glory Hole, drains vast areas of England and is regularly overflown by Spitfires and a Lancaster bomber—the River Witham.

Further Reading

Hadfield, Charles, *The Canals of Eastern England* (David & Charles). History.
Robinson, David N., *Lincolnshire Boats and Bridges in Camera* (Quotes Ltd, 1989; ISBN 0-86023-365-0). Old photographs.

Useful Contacts

British Waterways Manager responsible for the navigation of the river. Tel: 01636 705584.
Inland Waterways Association Tel: 01469 530138.

Boat-Hire

Adventure Afloat Tel: 01205 871439. Per day from Boston and Lincoln, also on the Navigable Drains.

Boat Trips

Maritime Leisure Cruises Tel: 01205 460595. From Boston, one-hour river trips on Wednesdays, pm. Also pre-booked cruises into The Wash and on the Witham.

Angling (Main clubs, page 207)

A popular fishery, has been used for National Championships. Bream, roach, perch, eels.
A free leaflet, *The Fens: Angling Opportunities*, is available from Boston Tourist Information, see below.

Public Transport

Nearest Rail Stations Lincoln, Boston.

Places to Visit in the Area

Tourist Information Boston. Tel: 01205 356656. Woodhall Spa. Tel: 01526 353775 (summer only).
Cycle Hire Jubilee Park, Woodhall Spa. Tel: 01526 52448. Signposted Spa and Woodhall Trails, or go as you please through Lincolnshire flat countryside.
Boston Market days—Wednesday, Saturday. Open-air auction Wednesdays in Wide Bargate.

Maud Foster Mill Tallest working windmill in England, seven floors and wholemeal shop. Not open every day. Tel: 01205 352188.

St Botolph's Church, 'The Stump' Views of one third of Lincolnshire from the outside gallery at the top of the 272ft tower. Guided tours. Tel: 01205 362864.

Sibsey Trader On the Navigable Drains. Working six-sail windmill, open to public in the summer. Tel: 01205 750036.

Lincolnshire Aviation History Comprehensive leaflets are available from Sleaford Tourist Information. Tel: 01529 414294.

The Battle of Britain Memorial Flight RAF Coningsby. Tel: 01526 344041. Spitfires, Hurricane and the only flying Lancaster bomber. The aircraft are sometimes away at shows, check in advance to avoid disappointment.

The Erewash Canal

Navigable; 12 miles long; 14 wide locks
OS map: Landranger sheet 129

MUCH OF *the character of any waterway is defined by the area through which it passes, and the Erewash reflects the pattern-less nature of a valley affected by centuries of exploitation. That doesn't mean the canal is unpleasant, but years of upheaval have left a blurred picture and an overall description is elusive.*

The waterway follows the Erewash valley, often alongside the river of the same name, through an area so rich in coal the canal could hardly fail to make the tremendous profits it did for its backers. Over the centuries that wealth attracted the railways and industry, both of which had an adverse affect on the appearance of the area.

The enormity of the Erewash Canal's successful past is the root cause of its somewhat jaded present.

THE jewel in the Erewash crown, at least for casual visitors, is the area at its southern end known as Trent Lock—a popular spot for weekend outings because it is a great waterway junction: the River Trent flows from west to east, the Erewash comes down from the north, and the River Soar arrives from Leicester and the South. The Navigation Inn has tables on its riverside lawns, further picnic tables are on the grassy banks by the junction, and many boats may be seen on the Trent and moored along the Erewash Canal. Early mornings are quiet: groups of fishermen arriving, a few boats on the move, waterbirds checking their

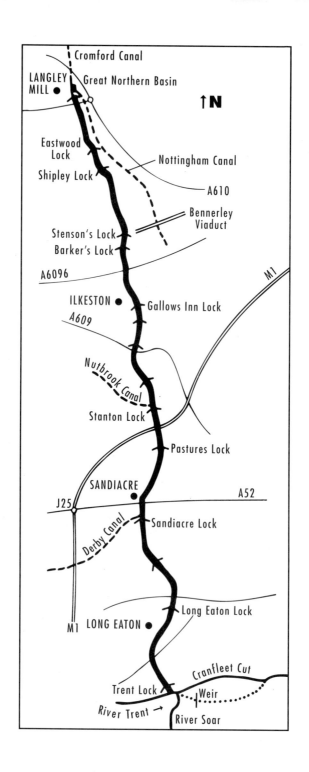

*Trent Lock: examples of the wide
variety of craft which may be seen*

territories for another day. On sunny afternoons families arrive, picnics are unpacked and an increasing number of boats are watched as they cruise by on the river or pass through Trent Lock itself—the first on the Erewash Canal.[1]

Crews operating the lock on a summer afternoon are usually watched by a crowd of gongoozlers, the attraction of boats being an age-old phenomenon. Nearby are the offices of the British Waterways' manager responsible for this and other canals in the area, a useful source of information, although closed at weekends. By the lock is the Steamboat Inn and one of the most incongruous signs on a canal pub—it shows a vessel looking like a steam-powered submarine! Yes, such vesels did exist.

Trent Lock is wide and like others that open out onto a river it does not have a by-wash, excess water from the canal flowing in a cascade from the top of the gates.

Above the lock the canal is often lined with boats—some pausing before cruising up the Erewash, others simply using the canal as a safe overnight mooring off the Trent. The area is quiet, except for an occasional passing train, and the towpath is wide, surfaced and grass-edged. The yard of Davison's Boatbuilders Ltd is on the far bank, surrounded by craft to be worked on and, in the summer, the buildings are aswoop with swallows. A little beyond is an unusual canal sight: a number of house-boats—not narrowboats that people are living on, but purpose-built floating dwellings; some are plain prefabricated oblongs, others are two-storey structures with balconies.

In addition to the house-boats, the far side of the canal is lined by all sorts of vessels, in among them the red-roofed Mills boatyard, established here in 1890 and using the dry-dock that once belonged to the Erewash Canal Company. This is a typical example of the continued use of facilities originally installed for the working boats that earned the canal's fat profits. Another is Sheet Stores Basin, the entrance to which is crossed by a towpath bridge. Now full of moored craft, it was originally used to tranship cargoes between boats and the railway that runs near the basin side. The name 'Sheet Stores Basin' is also a reminder of working days as it refers to the railway wagon tarpaulins once made there.

The two railway bridges near the basin mark a change in the canal's environment, the boats and boatyards giving way to the housing of Long Eaton and, after a while, traffic alongside on Tamworth Road (B6540). At least the canal is not hidden away and forgotten, and the stretch to Long Eaton Lock is pleasant—crossed by latticed footbridges and with tree-lined West Park on the far bank. By the lock is one of the

---

1. *Trent Lock—east of the M1, between Junctions 24 and 25. Lock Lane is off the B6540 at Sawley, signed 'Trent Lock'. Follow to end. Car park, toilets, by Navigation Inn.*

Lace mill near Long Eaton Lock

Sandiacre, with a typical ornate chimney of a lace mill

Sandiacre

177

lace mills which brought prosperity to the town and are a trademark of the Erewash Canal between here and Sandiacre. Mills they may be, but they are not dark, nor satanic, and I think they are rather attractive, especially their tall chimneys with ornate toppings. The mill by the lock is a long, three-storey building of pale pink brick, the many-paned windows that cover most of the canalside wall giving a welcome air of comradeship to the waterway rather than the exclusion often generated by mills in other areas.

From here the Erewash Canal continues on its way to the Langley Mill terminus, after Sandiacre often coming near to the border between Derbyshire and Nottinghamshire, which is formed by the river that shares the canal's name. Sometimes old and new industry closes in on the canal, in other areas old and new housing line its banks, elsewhere open fields give views of the gentle hills that edge the valley. Nothing lasts for long, however, nor develops the potential it promises; the canal improves the environment rather than the other way round but, having said that, it is worth exploring further as the canal has many interesting features.

At the end of Lock Lane—off the B6002 in the shadow of the over-flying A52—is Sandiacre Lock and the junction of the Erewash Canal and the Derby Canal. The bridge at the end of Lock Lane is the first on the Derby Canal, the infilled course of which extends between the housing. At the junction of the two waterways, and alongside Sandiacre Lock, is the only remaining tollhouse of the Erewash Canal Company, now the HQ of the Erewash Canal Preservation & Development Association (ECP&DA) and open to the public on Sunday afternoons. It's a pity about the traffic noise from the unseen A52, but otherwise it is pleasant, with lockside seats and grassy banks; and a short towpath walk into Sandiacre is worthwhile.

Once under and away from the A52, the canal becomes quieter, although in this busy valley roads are never far away. House gardens line the water's edge, looking across to the anglers dotted along the towpath. It's a wonder any fish survive in the Erewash Canal, considering the number of boys and men trying to catch them, not only week-end dabblers but also serious competition fishing organised by angling associations.

One of the plus-points that the Erewash does have is that it's not a canal that creeps unseen through built-up areas, as many waterways do. Instead the surrounding towns and suburbs use it to good effect and at Sandiacre, as at Long Eaton, the road comes alongside and local people are used to seeing boats moored by the bus stop. By the towpath Springfield Lace Mill forms a backdrop, its ornate chimney-top towering over the trees by the moorings. Past Sandiacre the view opens out over scrubby fields to distant gentle hills and rather nearer roads. Eventually the M1 swoops nearer and crosses over the canal before the waterway reaches the desolate area where the Stanton Ironworks used to be. Above Stanton Lock, two large pipes are the paltry remains of the junction with the Nutbrook Canal; with railway tracks running alongside the towpath, it's an industrial wilderness—once so busy, now unwanted and waiting for a future role.

Gallows Inn Lock is the start of the housing of Ilkeston and this continues for quite a distance, the canal skirting the edge of the town. Alongside Stenson's Lock[2] the impressive, delicate—and useless—Bennerley Viaduct stands as yet another of the area's monuments to an industrial past. Built to carry the long-gone Great Northern Railway, it now ends by the canal, the rest of the embankment cleared away for new housing. This is a scruffy area. The canal must be the only thing in sight that hasn't changed over the past two centuries; originally a controversial blight on the landscape itself, it now forms an unchanging corridor in a battered environment.

But all is not lost. Within another mile the canal breaks away from the buildings of Cotmanhay and at last finds some rural surroundings for much of its final mile to Langley Mill. By the time it reaches Shipley Lock, the canal is quiet and the gentle hills on the valley edge rise in the distance. The only road access is via a small lane, much of the traffic going to the nearby pub that has a restaurant and children's play area. The seat by the lock is often used by local people watching the boats pass through, and the towpath is a popular walking route. A few yards above the lock is an aqueduct, the canal crossing the River Erewash, here flowing attractively on its way to the Trent. Having at last achieved some degree of tranquillity, it is ironic that the canal should do so at a site that was once the busiest on the waterway.

On the far bank, the small field between the lock and the aqueduct was Dukes Wharf; coal-laden wagons used to run downhill from the local collieries along rail tracks that ended by the canal. Thousands of tons of coal were loaded onto boats each year, the busiest time being the first decades of the twentieth century, when water supply problems in the Nutbrook Canal meant that coal that had been transported on that waterway needed another outlet. Empty boats came up the Erewash, went through the lock to the wharf, loaded with coal and returned down the canal. It was so busy strict regulations were enforced to prevent congestion: no more than five boats could be above the lock at any one time, and empty craft could not wait any nearer than a certain point below the lock. It was not uncommon for sixty empty boats

2. *This lock is easily confused with Stenson Lock, not far away on the Trent & Mersey Canal.*

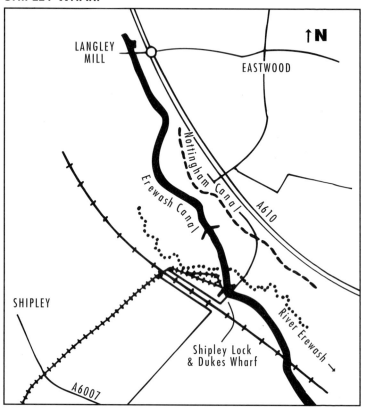

to be lined up along 900 yards of the canal. Eventually the railways took much of the trade, and in 1942 the last cargo of coal was carried from Dukes Wharf.

The path of the rail track can be walked, but little evidence remains of Shipley Lock's past activity—the canal is wide where the wharf used to be, and alongside the lock are two buildings, now renovated and private property; one was stables for boat-horses, the other a slaughter-house for injured pit-ponies.

Some sections of the towpath along the rest of the canal are well surfaced, others can be muddy after heavy rain. The path changes to the opposite bank at Eastwood Lock, the last of the canal's fourteen from the River Trent. Set into the ground, under the lock's name sign, is a plaque commemorating the nearby birthplace of novelist D.H. Lawrence. The Erewash River is across the fields that stretch from the towpath, eventually winding back to accompany the canal on its final yards, sometimes coming alongside the towpath. In the fields on the far bank can often be seen the route of the derelict Nottingham Canal, coming near to share the same terminus at Langley Mill. The easiest way to find the other canal is to make a short detour: a few yards beyond Eastwood Lock cross the footbridge (rope-marks on both corners) and take the track to an old brick bridge beneath which are the remains of the infilled Nottingham Canal with towpath alongside. Boats used to float where there is now grass, carrying coal direct to Nottingham to power the new mills and factories.

As the Erewash Canal arrives at its Langley Mill terminus, the countryside gives way to roads and commercial premises. Ahead, through a road bridge, can be seen the lock which is the last one on the Cromford Canal, built twenty years after the Erewash to link with it. So the Erewash Canal actually ends just below Langley Bridge Lock, but one crucial feature has still not been seen—a water supply! Water must be fed into a canal at its highest point; usually a stream flows in from a reservoir or river, but nothing obvious can be seen at Langley Mill. The answer is a lively bubbling in the canal by the towpath—water coming in from a pipe under the surface, water from the River Erewash.

Beyond Langley Bridge Lock is the Great Northern Basin and, even though it is part of the Cromford Canal, it is used at the moment as a turning point and moorings for boats reaching the end of the Erewash. The basin was restored by the volunteers of the Erewash Canal Preservation & Development Association (ECP&DA) in 1972–73 and they still do admirable work maintaining and improving the facilities. There are commemorative plaques and information boards galore, usually a mixture of moored boats, a roofed rack of stop-planks and a pumphouse for bringing water up from the river.

By the Great Northern Inn are further moorings, beyond a swingbridge. This arm of the basin is the northern end of the Nottingham Canal, the waterway seen derelict and infilled near Eastwood Lock. Crossing the swing-bridge and walking along the path is a good way of seeing the dry-dock of the Langley Mill Boat Company and perhaps a boat being repaired or improved.

The basin gives a focus to one end of a waterway that sometimes struggles to maintain a leisure identity; quite often it seems as if a boat loaded with coal is sure to come round the next corner. But it has many pleasant features and the waterways system would be much the poorer if everything was picture-postcard pretty. A reminder of why the system was built, and a waterway of character—that is the Erewash Canal.

Further Reading

Hadfield, Charles, *The Canals of the East Midlands* (David & Charles). History.
Waterways World, *Grand Union Canal* (Leicester Section) (1988;
ISBN 1-870002-20-2). Includes a cruising guide to the Erewash Canal.
See page 209 for address.

Useful Contacts

British Waterways Manager responsible for the Erewash Canal.
Tel: 0115 946 1017. Office by the side of Trent Lock.
Erewash Canal Preservation and Development Association
Tel: 0115 939 2339. Also: Lock Cottages, Lock Lane, Sandiacre,
Nottingham.

Boat Trips

Thompson's Boat Company River and canal cruises. Tel: 0115 972 5373.

Angling (Main clubs, page 206)

Very popular fishery. Roach, chub, gudgeon, bream, perch.

Public Transport

Rail Stations Langley Mill, Long Eaton.

Places to Visit in the Area

Tourist Information Nottingham. Tel: 0115 947 0661.
American Adventure. Theme park, rides, over 100 attractions in 200 acres of
parkland. Tel: 0773 531521.

The Horncastle Canal

Unnavigable; 11 miles long; 11 wide locks
OS map: Landranger sheet 122

TO BE pedantic, the Horncastle should not be called a 'canal'. For much of its eleven miles the waterway is an improved River Bain and as such would usually be called a 'navigation'. But it is an anomaly that's been handed down—so 'The Horncastle Canal' it is.

A waterway of quiet charm, although a superficial visit may fail to find it so. It doesn't go through spectacular scenery, it doesn't have a tourist 'honey-pot' like Lincoln to add interest, and it doesn't have any boats to watch because it's unnavigable, but a closer look will discover interesting locations at both ends and, inbetween, sites of past activity hidden in open Lincolnshire countryside.

To appreciate the Horncastle Canal a visitor needs unhurried time, and the talent to see clues which are often unobserved.

HORNCASTLE is a town that cannot ignore waterways. Developed by the Romans, the centre is situated on a narrow piece of land between two rivers, the Waring flowing into the Bain. In the 1790s Horncastle's wish for a navigable waterway to the Witham was achieved by improving the Bain and today much of the river's flow is taken down the canal's channel.

The canal does not go into the centre of the town. Instead boats used the two rivers to reach the busy wharves; along the Bain was the North Basin, along the Waring the South Basin. At a quiet time of the year,

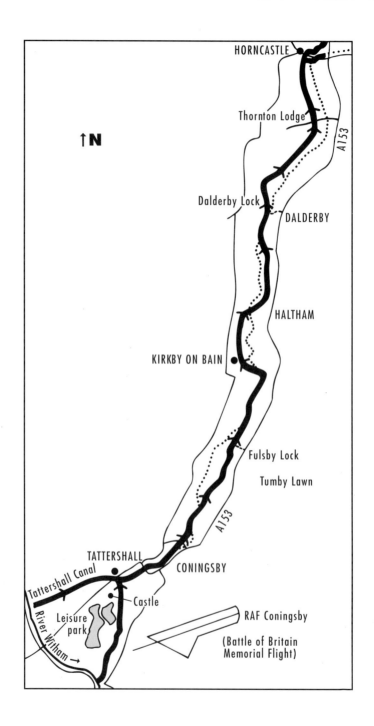

when the holiday traffic is not charging through to Skegness, it is very pleasant to park in the old Market Place and walk through the town discovering the evidence of past enterprise.

HORNCASTLE

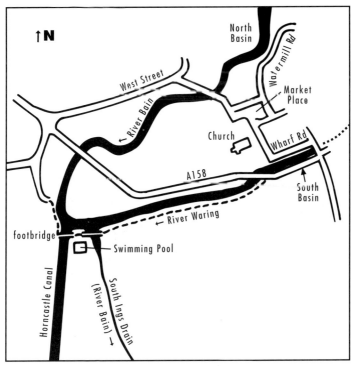

The name of Wharf Road is an obvious pointer and this was the site of the South Basin. The little River Waring now looks incapable of such a past but large amounts of corn and wool were loaded here, boatloads of coal were brought in and passengers embarked for trips to Boston or Lincoln. For instance, on 24th July 1854 the local brass band chartered the packet-boat *Hope* for a public day trip to Tattershall—to leave the South Basin at 8 am, fare one shilling:

> *... escape for a few hours the turmoil of the busy town. The band will enliven the voyage by a series of the most popular music of the day. A full Quadrille Band will be in attendance at Tattershall; Nectar and Ginger Beer may be had on board; Hot water for tea etc will be in readiness on the beach at Tattershall throughout the day, and ample provision will be made for the votaries of cricket, skittles, quoits, etc.*

Behind Wharf Road mellow old buildings are a reminder of the busy warehouses and commercial premises that used to fill the area. Nearby is The Ship public house, this can be seen in old photographs of the basin. The footpath along the river is where horses pulled the boats to and from the wharf, and the swimming pool was once the canal company's dry-dock. Outside the Waring meets the Bain; some of their waters going down the South Ings Drain, but the majority diverted along the canal.

Junction of the Rivers Bain and Waring at Horncastle

The Bain cannot be walked in the same way as the Waring, but by returning via West Street and Bridge Street it is possible to see many buildings that edge the riverbank and bear signs of past commercial use. There's a blue plaque where Bridge Street crosses the river that states this was the North Basin but, although this was a busy site, the head of navigation was further on, reachable on foot via the Market Place.

The area around the North Basin was the most industrialised part of the town—with tanneries, coal yards, bone dealers, boat builders, wool and corn warehouses, salt and lime merchant's sheds, and fishmongers. Now there's a supermarket car park.

Normally both rivers are shadows of their former self, modern drainage and flow controls keeping them in check—normally, but not always. The Bain and the Waring have always been variable in mood, and the wall plaque by Wharf Road shows the water level of the disastrous 1960 floods. More recently, I have walked beside them on an autumn Sunday in 1993, the water shallow, placid and crystal clear at the bottom

Old mill buildings by Horncastle's North Basin

of well-controlled channels. Two days later, after heavy rain, both rivers burst their banks and houses in West Street were flooded.

FROM HORNCASTLE the canal stretches straight into the distance, the northern section a true man-made waterway with the use of the Bain starting beyond Dalderby. The eleven miles to the River Witham are through rich farmland, and although the A153 takes the same route, it thankfully keeps a discrete distance while providing a convenient means of access. The sites of the first two locks can be seen from a side-road to Thornton Lodge; now sluices and water control points as are all the others on the canal. An information board by the cottage, at one end of The Spa Way footpath, tells of the neighbouring farm's activities and the significance of the cattle on the canal bank.

The importance of Dalderby in the canal's history is well disguised; today it is a small hamlet, but for a short period 200 years ago it was bustling with activity. The canal was built from the River Witham in the south, and by the time the navvies reached Dalderby the canal company had run out of money, still three miles short of Horncastle. For five years this remained the head of navigation and a busy wharf developed with goods transported from and to Horncastle by road. This traffic was controlled by a wharfinger for whom a cottage was built; now next to the Dalderby lay-by on the northbound A153 and called 'Navigation Farmhouse'.

The canal is reachable from a public footpath a few yards further along the road, by a war memorial. A by-product of stopping to look for waterways is often the discovery of other indications of the past. The war memorial at Dalderby made me remember that although I was looking for signs of two centuries ago, other events had touched the tiny hamlet since then. The handsome monument has twelve names on it, all from the First World War—twelve names; Dalderby only has eleven homes.

A gate leads to a meadow, on the far edge of which is an ancient ford across the River Bain to the village of Roughton. Beyond, via a bridge, is the canal. The old lock chamber is intact with recesses for the bottom gates and holes in the stonework for the paddle gear by the top gates. The wharf was below the lock, in the field between the canal and the wharfinger's cottage by the road. After five years the money was found to finish the canal and it was decided to build the remainder as an artificial channel rather than continue to use the Bain. Above Dalderby Lock the straight cut is very different to the winding Bain-based course of the rest of the canal where the two waterways continuously merge and diverge.

The Horncastle does not have a towpath that is a right of way so an OS map is required to explore it fully. Gently rolling countryside surrounds the canal and, south of Kirkby-on-Bain, flooded gravel pits give a background of various bird calls. The waterway edges past Coningsby, slipping quietly under the A153, innocently denying the sign on the bridge that says the canal/river destroyed the previous structure by washing it away in the 1960 floods.

Tattershall Castle (National Trust) is nearby. From the top of the tower Lincoln Cathedral can be seen to the west, Boston 'Stump' to the east. Although the River Witham links both locations, nothing of it can be

Tattershall Castle and the nearby church are widely visible across the flat landscape

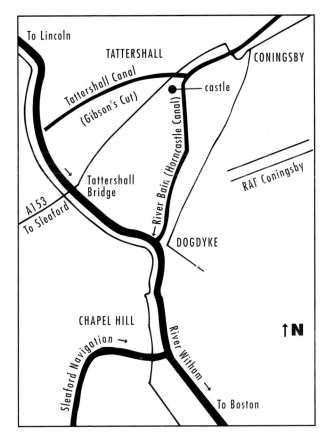

seen from the castle, and only one short stretch of the Horncastle Canal. There are marvellous views, especially of RAF Coningsby, but not of waterways.

Now we come to the part of the canal that has caused considerable confusion, many books continuing an error that is becoming widespread. To the north of the castle, the A153 crosses a man-made waterway, but this is not the Horncastle—it's the Tattershall Canal, also known as Gibson's Cut. This canal was built as a private venture a few years before the Horncastle; indeed its success prompted the promotion of the later waterway. The Tattershall Canal goes from the town to the River Witham, as does the Horncastle Canal and as a result many people have confused the two waterways.

The Tattershall Canal's embankment-blocked junction with the Witham is a little over half a mile upstream of Tattershall Bridge. A dent in a bend on the far bank of the Witham is the clue—just downstream of Holly Farm Caravan Park—and by standing on the road it is possible to see over the embankment to the straight line of the canal, water- and duck-filled and heading towards the distant castle.

The builders of the Horncastle Canal did not however use the Tattershall Canal in their route. Instead they continued to use the River Bain and met the Witham at Dogdyke, now a small community on a minor road, but in the past a busy water and rail transport centre. The Buccaneer pub and Hornblower's Restaurant have modern incongruous names, but The Packet Inn is a reminder of the packet-boats that used to call here on their trips up and down the Witham, and the ferry is remembered by Ferry Farm on the far bank. A small marina, hidden behind the buildings, is now the only reminder of the boating activity that once took place here, at the entrance to the River Bain and the Horncastle Canal.

Further Reading

Clark, J.N., *The Horncastle and Tattershall Canal* (The Oakwood Press, 1990; ISBN 0-85361-398-2).

Hadfield, Charles, *The Canals of Eastern England* (David & Charles). History.

Robinson, David N., *Lincolnshire Boats and Bridges in Camera* (Quotes Ltd, 1989; ISBN 0-86023-365-0). Old photographs.

Leaflet: *Lincolnshire Walks, Kirkby on Bain*. Available from Tourist Information.

Useful Contacts

Inland Waterways Association Tel: 01469 530138.

National Rivers Authority Lincoln. Tel: 01522 513100.

Public Transport

Rail Stations Nil.

Places to Visit in the Area

Tourist Information Horncastle. Tel: 01507 526636 (summer only).

Horncastle Small town with many old buildings and a busy market on Thursdays and Saturdays. Antique shops and second-hand bookshops.

Town Centre Trail A short walking tour of the town. Leaflet available.

Tattershall Castle Fifteenth-century brick tower keep, 100 feet high, wide views from the top. National Trust. Tel: 01526 342543.

Boats

WATCHING boats and ships is part of our national culture, perhaps an element of being an island race. On inland waterways this fascination is most common at locks; a phenomenon so widespread that there is a specific word to describe those who congregate to watch the boating activity—'gongoozlers'. No one knows where the term came from, although there are many differing opinions, but it is known to almost all the boaters who provide the entertainment. It is not a detrimental term; boaters themselves enjoy a good gongoozle when they are on land. There is just something about watching boats and ships.

The types of craft that can be seen on the waterways of this area are more varied than almost anywhere else—canoes and rowing-eights at Nottingham, narrowboats and cruisers almost everywhere, trip-boats at various places, racing yachts at Gainsborough, maintenance craft wherever they are needed, commercial barges on the Aire & Calder, sea-going ships on the River Trent.

Leisure Craft

Most of the leisure traffic is made up of cruisers and narrowboats—two distinct types of craft each with its own character. In general terms—it would need a volume of its own to cover this subject fully—cruisers are designed for use on rivers, narrowboats are a product of the canal system. No one has ever created a style of boat perfect for all uses; the variety of waterways in this area alone makes such a concept impossible.

Cruisers come in a great variety of sizes, from towering gin-palaces to little trail-boats towed to the water by car, but nevertheless they do

A river cruiser

have features in common. They are usually made of GRP (glass rein-
forced plastic), often called fibreglass. This makes them light and easy
to manoeuvre but not as tough as other vessels. Beneath the waterline
cruisers have a normal hull shape, giving them advantages in flowing
or deep water, the depth of boat under the water making them stable
and easy to control. They are not so suited, however, to narrow shallow canals, although small cruisers can cope quite well.

They are usually powered by petrol engines; on smaller cruisers these
are outboard at the stern. Such engines are good at acceleration and the
power they produce, for the light weight of such craft, gives cruisers a
lively performance.

A large percentage of the boats in this area are cruisers, as all but the
largest are suitable for nearly all of the waterways here, only the Chesterfield Canal having locks and bridges which may restrict access. In the
Midlands, however, it is different as narrow canals are predominant.

Narrowboats, on the other hand, have different characteristics. The first
thing to define is the name for such craft: they are narrowboats—not
longboats, not barges. 'Longboats' is incorrect because some of them
are quite short; 'barges' is mostly used for commercial craft carrying
bulk cargoes. 'Narrowboat' is correct because, although they can be
various lengths up to seventy feet, they are always narrow, only six
feet ten inches wide. The reason for such dimensions is that locks on
the early canals, such as the Chesterfield, were built to an agreed standard size: seventy feet long by seven feet wide. The bridges were also
made to a standard and the eighteenth-century canal boats were made
to fit—today's narrowboats are their modern descendants.

*A narrowboat. 'Longboat' is an incorrect term because,
although many are long . . . others are not.*

Narrowboats are usually made of steel, although some older types have wood or new fibreglass upperworks. Because they are designed for the shallow, still waters of canals, the bottom of the hull is flat. This originally allowed their working ancestors to carry about twenty tons of cargo without sinking very far into the water, and it still allows narrowboats to cruise all but the very shallowest of waterways. Their lack of height also clears bridges under which many cruisers cannot pass.

But, although there are few nooks and crannies of the waterways system that narrowboats cannot reach, they are not so good on deep, flowing waters. Their flat hulls do not cut through the water like conventional craft, but that doesn't mean they are unsafe: although they are out of their natural environment narrowboats cope very well. In this area they regularly cruise the tidal section of the River Trent, some even go across The Wash, although that needs expert advice, special planning, and perfect weather.

Almost all narrowboats have a diesel engine: strong, reliable, plodding units that will drive a heavy steel boat. Enthusiasts will go into raptures over the sound of old traditional engines, listening to them with a reverence never accorded the flashy petrol units on cruisers. This leads to another difference between the two types of boats. New cruisers are bought like cars—just choose the model you want and buy it complete. Narrowboats, on the other hand, can be purchased complete, or just a hull for the owner to fit out as required, or semi-complete with engine, plumbing, windows, outside painting, and only the interior for DIY. As a result, every narrowboat is different.

Interiors are as varied as houses. It is possible to have all mod cons, as much or as little as the owner wants or can afford—shower or bath, fridge, full-sized cooker, microwave, television, central heating, double bed; in fact many narrowboats are floating bungalows. Bottled gas and/or a generator powers most things, but it's quite common for a solid fuel burner to provide the heat for radiators and freshwater—that's why logs and tree branches can be seen on many cabin tops.

Within the group there are two main narrowboat styles: 'trad' (traditional) and, confusingly, 'cruiser'. Trads, as the name implies, are more like the old working boats: hardly any deck at the stern, the upperworks come almost to the tiller and the helmsman usually steers by standing in the cabin door, the engine-room being just within those doors. At the bows there is often a 'cratch', an upright panel that was originally used to secure the tarpaulins on the working boats. On the other hand, cruiser-style narrowboats, apart from their shape, have hardly any traditional features. They are a modern leisure design: a large deck at the stern so that more people can be outside; the engine is under the deck to save space; and there is an area in the bows for sitting outside.

The most noticed feature of all narrowboats is probably the bright paintwork: the traditional decoration is 'roses and castles' and geometric shapes, but nobody knows why. Some boaters like to have the designs as near as possible to the old styles, others are happy to have a modern equivalent. There are professional boat painters who specialise in such decoration, and many enthusiasts study the matter in great detail—others use Dulux and plastic lettering. Not only the boats are painted—lamps, water-cans, flower-tubs, kettles, anything and everything. Brasswork is found on chimneys and tillers, fancy ropework on steps. In general terms, narrowboats allow their owners to stamp their own personality on the craft much more than is possible with river cruisers.

Yachts are mainly seen on the larger rivers, especially the Trent and on the Witham at Boston. Inland waterways do not really have the width for sailing, and masts have to be lowered to pass under most bridges—so it is easier to put the sails away and start the engine. However, there is one occasion each year when yachts can be seen sailing and that is the 'Round the Island' race. Starting from Gainsborough, the yachts sail down the Trent, along the Humber, down the coast, into The Wash, up the Witham, along the Fossdyke, and down the Trent back to Gainsborough. They usually use their engines on the narrow Fossdyke, but there are penalties for the amount of fuel used so they use their sails as much as possible.

Hire-boats are usually narrowboats, of various lengths and layouts and they are a good way of getting afloat. The hire companies readily supply glossy brochures with all the details and, as with other holidays, the more you pay, the more you get in facilities and comfort. Boat-hire in

A traditional cratch on a modern narrowboat.

The two main types of narrowboats. Left: a 'cruiser' stern. Right: a 'trad' stern.

Buckby cans were used for drinking-water. Now they are often seen on narrowboat cabin-tops, painted with the traditional 'roses and castles' and the boat's name.

this area is listed at the end of each waterway's chapter. Page 209 has the titles of the inland waterway magazines which contain many advertisements for such holidays.

The booklet *Canal and River Cruising* from the Inland Waterways Association is a good overall introduction to boating—how to operate locks safely, the various rules of boating etiquette, how to avoid mistakes, and basic boat-handling.

Hotel-boats are craft which cruise throughout the system in England and Wales, they are the answer for people who wish to take a holiday afloat, but who do not relish doing the boat-handling 'work' themselves. Two narrowboats travel together; one has the passengers' sleeping accommodation in separate cabins, the other has the dining area, lounges, etc. for daytime use. The crew do all the chores, including the boat-handling and lock-operation, and guests can book for one or two weeks. Many people explore the inland waterways this way, including visitors from abroad, and the small number of passengers on each cruise makes a sociable mix. Details of companies operating hotel-boats can be found in the waterways magazines (see page 209).

Trip-boats operate from many places around the waterways system, these boats offer public trips of varying duration. Some are operated by professional companies, others by canal societies as a means of raising public awareness of a waterway. The boats differ in size from large river launches to small craft taking only twelve passengers. Nevertheless, they all give public access to the quiet pleasures of cruising rivers and canals. Details are listed at the end of each waterway's specific chapter.

Water Sports

The National Water Sports Centre is at Holme Pierrepont, Nottingham—at the side of the River **Trent**. Further details are on page 91.

Canoeing. This ranges from club meetings on narrow rural canals, to wide city centre rivers, to slalom courses marked by poles strung across a river. Canoe clubs often arrange summer weekend trips to quiet canals, pitching their tents in a nearby field.

Rowing and Sculling. Clubhouses edge the banks in towns and cities where tide-free wide water is available—Nottingham, Lincoln and Boston are examples. And yes, the coach can be seen, and heard, cycling alongside on the towpath, shouting through a megaphone at a sweating rowing-eight. It always looks like a scene from a 1950s film.

Commercial Craft

Barges still carry cargoes on the Trent, the Aire & Calder Canal and the Sheffield & South Yorkshire Navigation. When fully laden, they are low in the water, their size and capacity only apparent when one is seen empty and floating high. The operating companies specialise in heavy bulk cargoes, such as coal and gravel, taking advantage of the strong environmental lobby against road transport for such goods. It is a commercial world and contracts come and go, so it's not possible to say exactly where or when a barge may be seen. Occasionally working boats, for example sea-going tugs, use the Witham/Fossdyke link as a short cut between the Wash and the Trent.

Sea-Going Ships. On the River Trent sea-going ships reach upstream as far as Gainsborough, or to be more accurate Beckingham Wharf on the west bank opposite the town. They can also be seen at Keadby and other Trent wharves further downstream, and in Goole docks where the Aire & Calder Navigation meets the River Ouse. Many of the vessels are British, but the flags of other nations can be seen—Norway, Germany, Sweden, the Netherlands and Russia amongst them.

The ships that go as far as Gainsborough, all of eighty miles from the sea, are usually about sixty metres long. Many cargoes are timber from the Baltic, but rock salt and nitrates are also carried. Because of the many bends in the Trent, they usually have a local pilot on board and time their arrival and departure to coincide with the highest tides in the fortnightly cycle. Larger ships use the wharves further downstream near Keadby, where they deliver various cargoes including animal feed, pig iron, minerals, fertiliser, coke and chemicals.

The many basins of Goole docks give vessels shelter from the tides in the River Ouse, and supply the facilities for switching cargoes between the ships and the barges of the Aire & Calder Navigation.

Maintenance Boats. The variety of craft used to maintain the waterways seems to be endless—dredgers, tugs, pushers, piling boats, dumb-barges, floating cranes, weed and reed cutters can be seen throughout the network. Sometimes they are involved in a major project such as the virtual reconstruction of a lock, more often they are doing one of the thousands of minor tasks that constantly need attention.

British Waterways' vessels are now painted green instead of a rather insipid blue and their names are often indicative of the area in which they work; for example *Will Scarlet* is one of the fleet on the Nottingham & Beeston Canal.

A loaded tanker on its way to Goole, along the Aire & Calder Navigation

Many sea-going ships visit the busy Goole Docks

British Waterways little workboat,'Will Scarlet', at Nottingham

Various

Boat Shows and Rallies. Annual boat shows, rallies and festivals are a colourful part of the waterways scene throughout the summer. The waterways magazines contain the dates of all such events, the sizes of which range from extensive national shows to small local rallies to publicise a specific waterway. The most important is the Inland Waterways Association's national festival which is held at a different site each year. Considerable numbers of narrowboats attend and nearly every waterway organisation is represented in the adjacent tented area, including boat-builders with examples of their products. The largest event that is always in this area is the Nottingham Boat Show, held each year on the River Trent. This is a showcase for cruisers as well as narrowboats and is a good opportunity for the public to see every aspect of boating, the exhibitors coming from all over the country.

Branches of the Inland Waterways Association and Canal Societies organise small rallies and 'canal days', popular events that raise funds and public awareness of a local waterway.

Buying a Boat. The best advice is to hire a boat for a holiday before buying. That way the realities of boating will become evident, rather than the dreams, and different types of waterways and craft can be tried to see which is the most suitable. For example, some people love operating locks, others value the Norfolk Broads because they are lock-free; some find being out in the fresh air at the tiller of a narrowboat exhilarating, others prefer the interior comfort of a cruiser. Boating can give years of pleasure, but all can be ruined by an initial wrong purchase. If thinking of buying a new boat, then go to the boat shows and see what various builders have to offer. Also the waterways magazines are full of advertisements.

As with motoring there are hidden costs—insurance, licences, fuel and maintenance, with mooring fees an extra expense. Safety is also a consideration if young children are in the family. The Inland Waterways Association has various leaflets and booklets offering advice, as does British Waterways. The IWA's *Canal and River Cruising* is a good basic introduction to boating.

Plaques. Many narrowboats—and some cruisers—proudly bear a collection of metal plaques, either screwed to the cabin doors at the stern or covering the wall of the engine-room inside. These are testaments to places reached and events attended, each plaque inscribed with the relevant details. Some can be bought in canal-side shops by anyone, those are usually in the form of brasses as once worn by the boat-horses.

However, the most treasured are the plaques that can only be acquired by the boat reaching various places on the waterways system, especially the furthest points a boat can reach on little-used canals—the 'head of navigation'. These are sold by canal societies and waterway groups, but only on receipt of proof that the boat did reach the place claimed, usually a photograph. Another class of plaque which has to be earned, are those showing attendance at a boat show or rally.

VHF Radio. On the small sheltered inland waterways of the Midlands it is rare to find boats with VHF radios, but in this area many have them. This is because boats here are often cruising on tidal rivers, and on waterways where large fast-moving commercial vessels may be encountered. By listening to the radio communications of ships and barges it is often possible to have advance warning of their presence, and to keep safely out of the way! Also boat-handling can be a little difficult on fast-flowing tidal waters and it is of great benefit if a destination lock can be made ready before arrival—a simple matter via radio.

Boats without radios are monitored by lock-keepers noting the destination of each craft entering a tidal river, and passing the details to the relevant lock to check for arrival.

History

IF AN opinion poll asked people to name transport networks, the probable answers would be—road, rail, and air. Hardly anyone would say 'water'. That's understandable in our fast-moving society, but it's a response that would have baffled our ancestors. Throughout most of the recorded history of these islands—in round figures 2,000 years back to the Romans—water transport has been the most important system of all. Only in the last 140 years or so have the liquid highways been relegated to the heritage department.

Before railways and surfaced roads it was the great rivers that dominated society. The Romans, Vikings and all the other early invaders used the waterways to reach far inland, and then used the same routes to carry supplies to their garrisons. In more peaceful times, nearly all the nation's trade flowed along the rivers. Settlements developed into towns and cities, where the waterways could be crossed by bridge or ford, or at the furthest point upstream reachable by boats.

The roads were atrocious; we would hardly recognise them as such— deep mud when wet, deep ruts when dry, dusty, uneven, and narrow. Most goods were carried on packhorses because wheeled vehicles could often not cope with the conditions, but heavy loads could easily be carried by boat. The accepted solution was to carry land cargoes to the nearest navigable point on a river. By 1276 Bawtry on the River Idle was busy importing and exporting south Yorkshire's goods. Knottingley on the River Aire was the port for the output of the Aire and Calder valleys. Doncaster thrived as the navigable limit of the Don.

The waterways were crucially important as trade increased, and the delays to boat traffic caused by floods, shallows and acute bends became unacceptable. The result was centuries of gradual improvement, shallows were bypassed, depths were increased by weirs and locks, and the water was confined between higher banks and not allowed to spread over the surrounding land. In the 1620s Vermuyden, a Dutch engineer, drained the marshes between the Trent and the Ouse, and re-routed the Don and the Idle. By 1700 improvements on the rivers Calder and Aire had taken boats to Wakefield and Leeds. Seventy years later John Smeaton, of Eddystone Lighthouse fame, had engineered further upstream on the Calder and brought water transport to Sowerby Bridge, deep in the Yorkshire hills. The Trent and Witham had also been improved.

There was now a national system of river navigations, but this first phase of the water transport system had reached its peak. By the 1760s it was becoming evident that the rapid industrial changes taking place were generating new transport requirements. Coal needed everywhere. Unfortunately, the coalfields were not necessarily near the navigable rivers, and coal delivery by packhorse was woefully inadequate. Near Manchester the Duke of Bridgewater's solution was to take his coal to the new city by building an artificial river—the Bridgewater Canal. It was the dawn of the Canal Age.

Nevertheless, in north-east England the rivers did not lose their significance because the new canals were built to link into the existing system—a precedent set by the Romans when they dug the Fossdyke to connect the Witham and the Trent. Of the new era, the first 'artificial river' to be completed in this area was Huddersfield's Broad Canal in 1776, joining the town to the River Calder but only four miles long. The first real herald here of the new age was the Chesterfield Canal—by 1777 it had connected its name-town to the River Trent with 46 miles of channel, 65 locks, including 23 in staircase flights, two tunnels, one of which was over one and half miles long, aqueducts and a reservoir. It was a phenomenal engineering achievement—a product of an Industrial Revolution that was to change the world—and the rivers flowed on.

Commercial interests soon realised the potential of this new type of waterway and the Selby Canal and the Erewash Canal were both completed within the next two years. Before more work could be done, the financial and industrial fabric of the country was damaged by the trade restrictions and costs of the revolution in the American colonies. The 1780s were hard years for the canal engineers—no contracts on offer. But the 1790s were to be completely different, and provided more work than they could manage as 'canal mania' swept the land. In this area the decade saw the construction of the Cromford, Nottingham, Derby, Nutbrook, Grantham, Barnsley, and Horncastle canals, and the Slea Navigation—as well as major improvements on the Trent and the Witham. In addition, the Rochdale Canal and the Huddersfield Narrow Canal were built to link into the north-eastern system.

The next thirty years were the heyday of water transport, especially after 1815 when steam-powered boats became available and timetables could be adhered to. New travel opportunities were created when paddle-steamers and road coaches worked together to create a complex network of passenger services. The most popular in this area were the packet-boats from Selby, six days a week to Hull—the Trent steamers between Gainsborough and Hull, stopping at all riverside villages—and the road/river service between Sheffield, Doncaster and Hull. Other routes linked into these and in the 1830s there were so many steamboats on

Sailing keel passing through Keadby Lock, circa 1920
Reproduced by kind permission of Lincolnshire County Council, Recreational Services

the Trent and Humber that a 'companion' was published listing the services and facilities available.

Sheffield was eventually connected to this widespread system by a canal to the River Don, and the port of Goole was created when a new canal bypassed the lower reaches of the River Aire. At the same time further improvements were made to the rivers Trent, Don and Witham. But progress was accelerating. Canals and steamboats had augmented a river system that had been used for centuries, but now the engineering abilities that had made them possible was to go on to create a transport revolution. The Canal Age of the 1790s had been hectic enough, but it was as nothing to the 'railway mania' that was about to sweep the country—but the rivers flowed on.

At first the railways were used as feeders to the existing river/road systems, but eventually their tracks led to all towns and cities and the waterways finally lost their importance. The roads also improved and passengers and the majority of cargoes went ashore. The canals were abandoned and sometimes obliterated, the rivers were 'relegated' to their natural function of draining the land so that their competitors could thrive. Some waterways were large enough to keep bulk cargo carrying and these services still operate on the Trent, Ouse, and Aire & Calder Navigation. These are however the exceptions and elsewhere inland water transport gradually came to an end.

The 1950s and 1960s were dark days for the waterways; hardly anyone saw a use for remnants of another age. Then the leisure revolution came along and the potential of the rivers and canals was recognised on a wide scale. They have lost the central transport role they held for nearly 2,000 years, but today the rivers are being improved once more—this time with waterside paths, picnic areas, angling platforms, bird-watching hides, and boat moorings by pubs. The remaining canals have visitor centres, hire-boats, wildlife walks, information panels, landscaped locks, restaurants, guide-books, narrowboats and cruisers.

And what is lost is not lost forever; the 1990s have become the second Canal Age. There are navvies restoring canals and installing locks all over the place—Chesterfield, Sowerby Bridge, Sleaford, Grantham, Huddersfield, Barnsley and Derby. Other schemes are planned for Cromford and Horncastle. There is even the possibility that previously unnavigable sections of the rivers Dearne and Rother may see boats for the first time.

The future? Perhaps our current obsession with roads is a temporary aberration. Perhaps environmental pressures will create a renewed interest in water-borne transport. Whatever happens in the future—the rivers will flow on.

Angling

A NATIONAL Rivers Authority rod licence is required before fishing freshwater in England and Wales. It is available from most fishing tackle shops and Post Offices. However, the holder of a rod licence must still obtain the permission of the owner or tenant of the fishing rights. Details of the fish stocked are at the end of each chapter, but the main clubs on each waterway are listed below.

The rights on British Waterways and National Rivers Authority waters are licensed to angling clubs who control the day-to-day fishing on specified lengths. These clubs usually make their waters available to non-members by day permits, often sold on the towpath by a patrolling bailiff. Prices of day permits vary from 75p to £2 or so. If day permits are not available, signs at bridges will normally state that fishing is for members only.

Fishing is from the towpath and is not encouraged from boats as this may cause navigational hazards. Boats have priority at recognised mooring sites and no fishing at all may take place from lock landings, water points and waste disposal points. Also, please remember that walkers and cyclists are entitled to use the towpath and must not be obstructed with fishing tackle. The British Waterways' code of practice for anglers is available from any BW office.

Aire & Calder Navigation

Leeds & District Angling Association, 74 Stoney Rock Lane, Becketts St,
    Leeds LS9 7TB.
Boothferry Joint Angling Club, 39 Clifton Gardens, Goole DN14 6AR.

Calder & Hebble Navigation

Brighouse Angling Association, 1A Church Lane, Brighouse,
West Yorkshire HD6 1AT.
Bradford No. 1 Angling Association, 6 More Close Lane, Queensbury,
Bradford BD13 2BP.
Wakefield Angling Club, 29 Victoria Crescent, Horsforth, Leeds LS18 4PT.

Chesterfield Canal

East of Norwood Tunnel

Worksop & District Angling Association, 9 Edward Street,
Worksop S80 1QP.
Sheffield & District Angling Association, 1 Everingham Road, Longley,
Sheffield S5 7LA.
Retford Angling Association, 31 Ainsdale Green, Ordsall,
Retford DN22 7NQ.

West of Norwood Tunnel

At present not allowed, check with Derbyshire Ranger Service,
01246 866960.

Erewash Canal

Long Eaton Federation of Anglers, 75 College Street, Long Eaton,
Nottinghamshire.
Middleton Working Man's Club (Angling Section), 27 John Street, Ilkeston,
Derbyshire.
National Coal Board Angling Club, 27 Hardybarn, Shipley,
Derbyshire DE7 7LY.

Fossdyke Canal

A British Waterways direct-managed fishery, the BW bailiff sells day permits
on the bank.

Grantham Canal

Day tickets are available at the Nottingham end.

Nottingham & Beeston Canal

Nottingham Anglers Association, 95 Ilkeston Road, Nottingham NG7 3HA.
Nottingham Federation of Anglers, 17 Spring Green, Clifton Estate, Nottingham.

Selby Canal

Goole Angling Association, 39 Clifton Gardens, Goole DN14 6AR.
Selby Angling Association, 6 Cherry Tree Close, Brayton, Selby,
   North Yorkshire.

Sheffield & South Yorkshire Navigation

Sheffield & Tinsley Canal
Sheffield basin to Cadman St, no fishing. Details on the rest of the canal often
   change, the latest information is available from British Waterways
   (Newark), see page 112.

Don Navigation
Rotherham & District UAF, 91 Cherrytree St, Elsecar, Barnsley.
Doncaster & District AA, 28 Holmescarr Rd, Rossington, Doncaster DN11 0QF.
Pilkington AC, Pilkington Rec. Club, Old Kirk Sandall, Doncaster DN3 1HW.
Upstream of Mexborough, details from British Waterways (Newark), see page 112.

New Junction Canal
Doncaster & District AA. As above.

Stainforth & Keadby Canal
Stainforth & Keadby Joint Angling Committee, 13 Wesley Rd, Kiveton Park,
   Sheffield S31 8RJ.
Stainforth Town Council, Travellers Rest Farm, Norton, Doncaster DN6 9HF.
Stainforth AA, 79 Copley Crescent, Scawsby, Doncaster DN5 8QW.

River Witham

A free leaflet, *The Fens: Angling Opportunities*, is available from Boston Tourist
   Information, see page 171.
Witham & District Joint Angling Association, 30 Gunby Avenue,
   Lincoln LN6 0AW.
Boston & District Angling Association. Tel: 01205 350088.

General Contacts

British Waterways

Emergency Number for the public to report problems; phone the operator, ask for 'Freephone Canals', 24-hour coverage.

Customer Services Department Willow Grange, Church Road, Watford, Herts WD1 3QA. Tel: 01923 226422.

The local office responsible for a waterway is listed at the end of each chapter.

National Rivers Authority

National Emergency Number Tel: 0800 807060. For the public to report pollution, poaching, flooding problems. Free calls from anywhere, control room manned 24 hours.

Anglian Region Kingfisher House, Goldhay Way, Orton Goldhay, Peterborough PE2 0ZR. Tel: 01733 371811.

Northumbria & Yorkshire Region Rivers House, 21 Park Square South, Leeds LS1 2QG. Tel: 0113 244 0191.

Severn Trent Region Sapphire East, 550 Streetsbrook Road, Solihull, West Midlands B91 1QT. Tel: 0121 711 2324.

Inland Waterways Association

Head Office 114 Regent's Park Road, London NW1 8UQ. Tel: 0171 586 2556.

East Midlands Region 25 Bedford Avenue, Mansfield NG18 3AD. Tel: 01623 633895.

Lincolnshire & South Humberside Conifer Cottage, North End, Goxhill, South Humberside DN19 7JX. Tel: 01469 530138.

Nottingham, Leicester & Derby 3 Onchan Avenue, Carlton,
     Nottingham NG4 1DD. Tel: 0115 987 5475.
South Yorkshire & Dukeries 1 Vicarage Way, Arksey, Doncaster DN5 0TG.
     Tel: 01302 873127.
The local branch for a waterway is listed at the end of each chapter.

Canal Societies

Listed at the end of the relevant waterway chapters.

Waterways Magazines

Canal and Riverboat Monthly. A.E. Morgan Publications, Stanley House,
     9 West Street, Epsom KT18 7RL. Tel: 01372 741411.
Waterways World Monthly. Kottingham House, Dale Street,
     Burton-on-Trent DE14 3TD. Tel: 01283 564290.

Tide Tables

British Waterways, Mill Lane, Mill Gate, Newark NG24 4TT.
     Tel: 01636 704481. Price: £1.00, inc. p+p.

Aegre Schedule

Free from the National Rivers Authority, Severn Trent Region (see p. 208).

Trip-Boats/Hire-Boats

Listed at the end of the relevant waterway chapters.

Angling Clubs

See separate listing, page 205.

General

Canal Postcard Collectors Circle 93 Wish Hill, Willingdon,
     Eastbourne BN20 9HQ.
Towpath Action Group 23 Hague Bar Road, New Mills,
     Stockport SK12 3AT. Tel: 01663 742198.

General Bibliography

Books on specific waterways are listed at the end of the relevant chapter.

Boucher, Cyril T.G., *James Brindley, Engineer, 1716–1772* (Goose and Son Ltd, 1968).

Bowskill, Derek, *Northeast Waterways* (Imray Laurie Norie & Wilson, 1986; ISBN 0-85288-099-5). Navigational guide. Superseded by guides to specific waterways, see details at the end of the following chapters: Chesterfield Canal, Sheffield & South Yorkshire Navigation, Aire & Calder Navigation, Calder & Hebble Navigation.

Hadfield, Charles, *Hadfield's British Canals* (Alan Sutton Publishing, 1994; ISBN 0-7509-0017-2). General history.

Hadfield, Charles, and A.W. Skempton, *William Jessop, Engineer* (David & Charles, 1979; ISBN 0-7153-7603-9). Story of the engineer responsible for the construction of many navigations in this area.

Index

212